2020 EBAY SOURCING GUIDE

Best-Selling Brands Plus Liquidation Sources

By
Ann Eckhart

Table of Contents

INTRODUCTION 1

CHAPTER 1: BABIES & KIDS.. 6

CHAPTER 2: BOOKS & MEDIA..13

CHAPTER 3: CAMERA & PHOTO 19

CHAPTER 4: CELL PHONES & ACCESSORIES....................31

CHAPTER 5: CLOTHING & ACCESSORIES........................38

CHAPTER 6: COLLECTIBLES..101

CHAPTER 7: ELECTRONICS..107

CHAPTER 8: CRAFTS:..111

CHAPTER 9: HEALTH & BEAUTY....................................115

CHAPTER 10: HOME & GARDEN:....................................149

CHAPTER 11: JEWELRY..174

CHAPTER 12: SPORTING GOODS....................................203

CHAPTER 13: TOYS & HOBBIES......................................217

BONUS: LIQUIDATION SOURCES 237

CONCLUSION..244

ABOUT THE AUTHOR..245

INTRODUCTION

I have been selling on Ebay since 2005 and writing books about how to make money on the site since 2013. The number one question I am asked on a nearly daily basis is "What sells on Ebay?". If you've been wondering that yourself, then this is the book for you!

There are a lot of "BOLO" ("Be On the Look Out for") lists and videos available online that tell you the supposedly hottest items to source to resell on Ebay. A true "BOLO" is a rare piece, something that you might stumble across one day that will bring in a good profit. However, "BOLO's" typically do not pay the bills. They tend to be hard to find and can take awhile to sell. What seasoned resellers are on the lookout for are the items and brands that are in demand TODAY. They want to find things that will sell quickly for a decent return on investment. These items are often referred to as "bread and butter" as they might not be exciting or flashy, but they sell fast and make sellers money.

This book contains the items that Ebay customers are currently searching for and buying in the major categories. Note that "major category" distinction as there are categories I've left out, such as vehicles, heavy machinery, and specialty equipment. I've focused on the items that are frequently found at garage sales and thrift stores and that are also relatively easy to ship. I know that I'm not sourcing and shipping treadmills and refrigerators on Ebay; I'm picking up books, clothing, and smaller items that sell fast and ship easily.

How To Read This Book: Each chapter features one main Ebay category with several subcategories. Most subcategories break down between brand new and used (secondhand). However, not all do. For instance, selling used cosmetics (unless they are vintage) is prohibited on Ebay; therefore, the makeup brand lists are all for new items. If I only provide one subcategory condition, it means that data wasn't available to support the opposite condition or that the item is prohibited to sell used. Most lists contain the top 10 items, although a handful have one or two more or less. The lists are in order of buyer demand.

Prices: I decided to omit pricing from this book as what an item ends up selling for varies dramatically based on condition, version, size, style, color, etc. I initially thought about including averages; but even those numbers were significantly off when considering all of the variables. While the brands listed are currently the best sellers, the fact that they are on the lists doesn't mean they are bringing in the most money.

New vs. Used: I decided to break most of the subcategories into "new" and "used". One would assume that brand new items are always the most in demand and sell more than secondhand ones, but that isn't always the case. Sometimes a used item is one that is no longer being produced, making it more valuable that its new counterpart.

Condition: One of the biggest factors in how much an item sells for is its condition. A barely worn sweater in a larger size will bring in much more money than a flawed tee shirt in an extra small. Just because you find a brand on one of the lists doesn't mean it will sell well if it has major condition issues, is out of style, or is in an undesirable size.

Brands Not Listed: Just because an item or brand didn't make a list doesn't mean that it doesn't sell well on Ebay. In fact, a brand that isn't listed could very well bring in much more money than the ones on the lists. However, the brands listed in this book are the current TOP sellers, the ones buyers are searching for and ultimately buying faster than other brands on the site.

Missing Categories: I mentioned that I omitted large items such as vehicles and power equipment, but there are also some subcategories that I was unable to provide statistics for. For instance, I was able to narrow down a ranking of fiction books by author; but since new books are constantly being released, I found it pointless to provide a list of the current best sellers as that list changes daily. The same goes for toys. While I was able to find some lists for certain toy brands and type, I wasn't able to narrow down the best-selling games or dolls as those change monthly, if not weekly. While L.O.L. Surprise Dolls may be hot right now, a completely new toy could knock it off the charts at any time.

Research: This book is meant to be a basic sourcing guide; it is designed to help you familiarize yourself with multiple categories and brands so that you know what to look for when sourcing. As an Ebay seller, it's important to always do your own research. Before I list anything, I do a completed listing search for the item on Ebay to see how to best price it. There are also some items that may seasonal; while you can get top dollar for coats in the Fall and Winter, they are hard to sell in the Summer. This book is a guide; it's meant to give you some extra knowledge while sourcing, but you'll always want to do your own research to make sure an item is worth buying to resell.

Liquidation: While the bulk of Ebay sellers source their items from thrift stores and garage sales, you can also purchase products from liquidation companies. Therefore, I've provided a bonus chapter where I list the top liquidation companies that sell items you can resell on Ebay.

Again, this sourcing guide is just that: a guide. It's meant to open your eyes up to new items and brands that you may not already be familiar with. And it will hopefully make you reconsider some things you've been passing up. So many factors go into generating an Ebay sale, including:

- The condition, size, style, color, and/or brand of the item
- Creating a keyword loaded title for the listing
- Listing the item in the correct category
- Providing lots of crisp, clear photographs of the item from every angle
- Filling out the provided item specifics fields
- Disclosing any flaws
- Pricing the item competitively, including shipping costs

- Fast and professional shipping

- Providing excellent customer service, such as responding to customer questions, and working to resolve issue

I have personally learned so much from compiling this book. It's definitely changed the way I source items to sell on Ebay; and I hope it will for you, too!

CHAPTER 1

BABIES & KIDS

Clothing for babies and children can be difficult to sell on Ebay. The best way to resell kids' clothing is to sell it in like-size lots. However, the brands listed below do sell on their own. Remember, though, that condition, size, style, and color all factor in to whether anything, including children's clothing, will sell on Ebay. Baby items in particular are part of frequent recalls, hence why the only equipment I cover in this chapter are baby monitors. Finally, only some clothing categories are included; this doesn't mean other categories don't sell, but that they don't sell particularly well. For instance, parents look to Ebay for nice girls' dresses, not basic girls' tops.

Baby Monitors:

1. Infant Optics

2. Motorola

3. Summer Infant

4. Samsung

5. Vtech

6. Owlet

7. Levana

8. Angelcare

9. Sony

Baby Shoes - New:

1. Nike

2. Stride Rite

3. Native

4. VANS

5. Jordan

6. Salt Water Sandals

7. Crocs

8. Livie & Luca

9. Converse

10. Freshly Picked

Baby Shoes – Used:

1. Keen

2. Salt Water Sandals

3. Nike

4. Converse

5. Jordan

6. VANS

7. Crocs

8. Livie & Luca

9. Stride Rite

10. Freshly Picked

Boys' Clothing Sizes 4 & Up - New:

1. Vineyard Vines

2. Nike

3. Polo Ralph Lauren

4. Ralph Lauren

5. Lacoste

6. Under Armour

7. Tommy Hilfiger

8. True Religion

9. Adidas

10. Brooks Brothers

Boys' Clothing Sizes 4 & Up – Used:

1. Under Armour

2. Vineyard Vines

3. Nike

4. Ralph Lauren

5. Mini Boden

6. Polo Ralph Lauren

7. Hanna Andersson

8. Crewcuts

9. Lacoste

10. Brooks Brothers

Boys' Shoes – New:

1. Adidas

2. Jordan

3. Nike

4. Under Armour

5. Reebok

6. Khombu

7. Vans

8. Keen

9. Sperry

10. Stride Rite

Boys' Shoes – Used:

1. Keen

2. Nike

3. Under Armour

4. Vans

5. Heelys

6. Jordan

7. Ariat

8. Adidas

9. Sperry

10. Merrell

Girls' Dresses Size 4 & Up – New:

1. Lularoe

2. Matilda Jane

3. Lilly Pulitzer

4. Dollcake

5. Hanna Andersson

6. Janie and Jack

7. Ralph Lauren

8. Tea Collection

9. Gap

10. Crewcuts

Girls' Dresses Size 4 & Up – Used:

1. Lilly Pulitzer

2. Matilda Jane

3. LuLaRoe

4. Mini Boden

5. Tea Collection

6. Janie and Jack

7. Crewcuts

8. Justice

9. Hanna Andersson

10. Eleanor Rose

Girls' Shoes - New:

1. Michael Kors

2. KEEN

3. Stride Rite

4. Gymboree

5. Native

6. Birkenstock

7. Jordan

8. VANS

Girls' Shoes – Used:

1. Keen

2. Chaco

3. Ariat

4. Nike

5. Crocs

6. Teva

7. Mini Melissa

8. Converse

9. Salt Water

10. Birkenstock

CHAPTER 2

BOOKS & MEDIA

Books, CD's, DVD's, Blu-rays, and vinyl records aren't just for Amazon; these media items can sell quite well on Ebay! Following are the top authors, artists, and genres in each major category. Note that I'm not including average sale prices in this chapter as age, title and condition factor heavily into the sale price of media. This chapter instead serves as a guide to what authors and genres to be on the lookout for.

As I mentioned, condition factors heavily in to how much an item will actually sell for. Hardcover books tend to sell better than paperback; and entire series sets (books and television shows) are always sought after. For example, the complete Harry Potter series brand new in hardcover sells for an average of $93 with a used set bringing in $58.

Also, older hardcover book copies with dust jackets often sell better than a newer release. Most fiction books are first released in hardcover but are eventually switched to paperback. A first-edition Kristin Hannah hardcover may fetch you over $31 while a current paperback book from her will only sell for around $6.

Finally, one category not listed is Vintage Cookbooks. There are old cookbooks, both hardcover and paperback, can bring in over $150. A favorite of mine to resell are the vintage 3-ring binder hardcover Betty Crocker cookbooks, which, in excellent condition, can sell for nearly

$100. Since there are fewer copies of these cookbooks, and since condition and year of publication both factor heavily into how much they will sell for, there wasn't enough data to compile a separate list for them.

Fiction & Literature by Author (New Copies):

1. Kristin Hannah

2. Stephen King

3. J.K. Rowling

4. George R.R. Martin

5. Paulo Coelho

6. James Patterson

7. Dan Brown

8. Margaret Atwood

9. Brandon Sanderson

10. J.R. Ward

Fiction & Literature by Author (Used Copies):

1. George Orwell

2. F. Scott Fitzgerald

3. Ray Bradbury

4. Stephen King

5. J.D. Salinger

6. Margaret Atwood

7. Anthony Doerr

8. Diana Gabaldon

9. Paulo Coelho

10. Kristin Hannah

Non-Fiction Subjects:

1. Religion & Spirituality

2. Games & Puzzles

3. Self-Help

4. True Crime

5. Hobbies & Crafts

6. Paranormal & Metaphysical

7. Law & Government

8. Transportation

9. History

10. Collecting

Magazine Top Subjects – New Copies:

1. Humor & Satire

2. Religion & Spirituality

3. News

4. Medicine

5. Hobbies & Crafts

6. Music

7. Movies & TV

8. Art & Photography

9. Celebrity

Magazine Top Subjects (used copies):

1. Gay & Lesbian

2. Antiques & Collectibles

3. Teen

4. Video

5. Game

6. Men's Interest

7. General Interest

8. Art & Photography

9. Agriculture

10. Women's Interest

11. Humor & Satire

Vinyl Records – New:

1. Frank Ocean

2. Taylor Swift

3. Childish Gambino

4. Pink Floyd

5. Chance the Rapper

6. Samhain

7. Grateful Dead

8. Nirvana

9. Redd Kross

10. Metallica

Vinyl Records – Used:

1. Grateful Dead

2. Black Sabbath

3. Pink Floyd

4. Ozzy Osbourne

5. Steely Dan

6. Def Leppard

7. Samhain

8. Led Zeppelin

9. Metallica

CHAPTER 3

CAMERA & PHOTO

If you frequently attend estate sales, you'll likely stumble upon a lot of camera equipment. This was another tricky chapter to provide detailed information for as the vast number of camera types is staggering. Canon, for instance, makes basic models as well as high-quality professional pieces; and the resale prices can vary from a few bucks to thousands of dollars. Overall, I find the demand for secondhand, especially vintage, cameras to be much greater than the new models. Once a camera is out of production, its value tends to increase. Being able to test a camera weighs heavily into how much you'll be able to charge for it. Following are the best-selling brands in each subcategory.

Binoculars – New:

1. Nikula

2. Vortex

3. Bushnell

4. Perrini

5. Night Owl Optics

6. Vivitar

7. Nikon

8. Bestguarder

9. Swarovski Optik

Binoculars – Used:

1. Nikon

2. Bushnell

3. Canon

4. Carl Zeiss

5. ZEISS

6. Steiner

7. Swift

8. Bausch + Lomb

9. Minolta

Camcorders – New:

1. GoPro

2. Samsung

3. Xiaomi

4. Activeon

5. Flip Video

6. Google

7. DB Power

8. Campark

9. 360Fly

10. Vivitar

Camcorders – Used:

1. GoPro

2. Sony

3. Canon

4. Samsung

5. Blackmagic Design

6. Panasonic

7. Sharp

8. Flip Video

9. JVC

10. Kodak

Camera Batteries - New:

1. GoPro

2. Nikon

3. Canon

4. Wein

5. Sony

6. Fujifilm

7. Panasonic

8. Garmin

9. Vivitar

10. Wasabi Power

Camera Bags - New:

1. Altura Photo

2. f-stop

3. Peak Design

4. Neewer

5. Conta

6. Lowepro

7. Smatree

8. Canon

9. Nikon

10. Leica

Camera Bags – Used:

1. Pelican

2. Think Tank Photo

3. Lowepro

4. Peak Design

5. Tamrac

6. Canon

7. Nikon

8. Tenba

Camera Memory Cards:

1. Transcend

2. Cisco

3. Panasonic

4. Olympus

5. Sony

6. SanDisk

7. FujiFilm

8. SmartMedia

9. Lexar

10. Kingston

Digital Cameras – New:

1. Polaroid

2. Vivitar

3. Samsung

4. Kodak

5. Ricoh

6. Crayola

7. Olympus

8. Intova

9. Fujifilm

Digital Cameras – Used:

1. Canon

2. Panasonic

3. Sony

4. Nikon

5. Fujifilm

6. Kodak

7. Olympus

8. Samsung

9. PENTAX

10. Leica

Instant Film:

1. Fujifilm

2. Polaroid

3. Kodak

4. Nikon

5. Lomography

6. Agfa

Film Cameras – New:

1. Nikon

2. Holga

3. Nishika

4. Lomography

5. Leica

6. Canon

7. Hasselblad

8. Fuji

9. Olympus

Film Cameras - Used:

1. Olympus

2. Canon

3. Fujifilm

4. Nishika

5. Mamiya

6. Nikon

7. Pentax

8. Yashica

9. Contax

10. Graflex

Camera Flashes:

1. Neewer

2. Holga

3. Nikon

4. Sunpak

5. Nishika

6. Viltrox

7. Canon

8. Altura Photo

Camera Filters - New:

1. Neewer

2. Schneider

3. Vivitar

4. Hoya

5. Nikon

6. LEE Filters

7. GoPro

8. Tiffen

9. Zomei

10. Schneider Optics

Camera Filters – Used:

1. Nikon

2. Leica

3. Hoya

4. Rollei

5. Canon

6. Tiffen

7. Contax

8. Pentax

Camera Lenses - New:

1. Industar

2. Helios

3. Mamiya

4. Jupiter

5. Yongnuo

6. Panasonic

7. Fujinon

8. Canon

9. Fujifilm

10. Neewer

Camera Lenses – Used

1. Canon

2. Sony

3. Nikon

4. Fujifilm

5. Panasonic

6. Sigma

7. Tamron

8. Olympus

9. Mamiya

10. Helios

Camera Stabilizers – New

1. Zhiyun

2. GoPro

3. DJI

4. Steadicam

5. SmallRig

6. FeiYu

7. Sony

8. Neewer

Camera Stabilizers – Used

1. DJI

2. Zhiyun

3. FeiYu

4. Glidecam

5. GoPro

6. Roxant

7. Sony

8. Freefly

CHAPTER 4

CELL PHONES & ACCESSORIES

Just like cameras, the sheer number of cell phone models is astronomical. With Chinese online sellers offering parts and accessories for as little as a penny on Ebay, and with these items being sold at every big box retailer in America, cell phones and accessories can be a tough sell. iPhones are, not surprisingly, the best-selling brand of phone. When sourcing cell phone parts and accessories to resell on Ebay, I stick to brand new and sealed items. However, if you are skilled at testing and repairing electronics, there is definitely potential for you to make money. Note that some brands, such as Otterbox, don't allow you to list their items as new on Ebay's site, even if they are. When I list Otterbox products, I list them as "open box".

Cell Phone & Smartphone Parts:

1. Covers

2. LCD Separators

3. Touch Screens

4. Frames

5. LCD Screens

6. Assembly Kits

7. Screen Digitizers

8. Screen Glass

9. Logic Boards

10. Printed Circuit Boards

11. Tool Kits

Cell Phone & Smartphone Parts for Brands:

1. Apple

2. LG

3. ZTE

4. Verizon

5. Samsung

6. Google

7. OnePlus

8. ASUS

9. Motorola

10. Xiaomi

Cables & Adapters: iPhone compatible cases and adapters are the most sought after

Cases, Covers & Skins – New:

1. LifeProof

2. Pelican

3. Otterbox

4. Kate Spade New York

5. Mophie

6. Tech21

7. Speck

8. Apple

9. Michael Kors

Chargers & Cradles – New:

1. Samsung

2. Anker

3. Xiaomi

4. Tzumi

5. Apple

6. Belkin

7. X-Dragon

8. Blackweb

9. Mophie

Chargers & Cradles – Used:

1. Anker

2. Apple

3. Samsung

4. Belkin

5. Motorola

6. RAVPower

7. Mophie

8. PhoneSoap

9. Verizon

Screen Protectors – New Only:

1. Fosmon

2. Otterbox

3. Zagg

4. Spigen

5. Case-Mate

6. OnePlus

7. Ringke

8. Insten

9. Sonix

10. Qmadix

Signal Boosters – New:

1. T-Mobile

2. Cisco

3. Nextivity

4. Sprint

5. weBoost

6. AT&T

7. Samsung

8. Wilson

9. Verizon

Signal Boosters – Used:

1. Cisco

2. AT&T

3. Samsung

4. Wilson

5. Verizon

6. Cel-Fi

7. SureCall

8. zBoost

Headsets:

1. Apple

2. LG

3. Skullcandy

4. Joway

5. Parrot

6. Anker

7. Plantronics

8. Bose

9. Xgody

10. BlueParrot

11. Blue Tiger

12. Motorola

Smart Watches - New:

1. Apple

2. Samsung

3. Kingwear

4. LG

5. Motorola

6. Pebble

7. Nike

8. Fitbit

9. Xiaomi

10. Misfit

Smart Watches – Used:

1. Apple

2. Samsung

3. LG

4. ZTE

5. Pebble

6. Nike

7. Motorola

8. ASUS

CHAPTER 5

CLOTHING & ACCESSORIES

Clothing is the largest category on Ebay with dozens of subcategories. Styles change frequently, but the brands in this chapter have proven to be the current best sellers. However, remember that just because a brand isn't listed doesn't mean it won't sell. And just because these brands are listed doesn't mean they are the most profitable. These are just the most searched for and purchased brands of clothing currently on Ebay. While there are some high-end designer labels that I know I myself will likely never find in my area, these lists all contain several brands that can be sourced anywhere in the country.

Men's Bag Styles:

1. Fanny/Waist Pack

2. Military Bag

3. Leg Bag

4. Messenger/Shoulder Bag

5. Toiletry Bag

6. Crossbody Bag

7. Backpack

8. Duffle/Gym Bag

9. Travel Bag

Men's Bags – New:

1. Supreme

2. Oakley

3. Coach

4. Harley-Davidson

5. Tumi

6. The North Face

7. Tommy Hilfiger

8. Ralph Lauren

9. Nike

Men's Bags – Used:

1. Tumi

2. Supreme

3. Coach

4. Oakley

5. Jack Spade

6. Samsonite

Men's Belts – New:

1. Gucci

2. Salvatore Ferragamo

3. Nike Golf

4. Hermes

5. Harley-Davidson

6. Coach

7. Fendi

8. 5.11 Tactical

9. PGA Tour

Men's Belts – Used:

1. Salvatore Ferragamo

2. Allen Edmonds

3. Fendi

4. Gucci

5. Vineyard Vines

6. Coach

7. Louis Vuitton

8. Polo Ralph Lauren

9. Harley-Davidson

10. Orvis

Men's Hats - New:

1. Patagonia

2. Polo Ralph Lauren

3. Harley-Davidson

4. Gucci

5. Balenciaga

6. Under Armour

7. Jeep

8. Nike

9. Jordan

Men's Hats – Used:

1. Patagonia

2. Polo Ralph Lauren

3. Lauren

4. Stetson

5. Harley-Davidson

6. Supreme

7. Resistol

8. Nike

9. Ralph Lauren

10. Kangol

11. Sports Specialties

Men's Sunglasses – New:

1. Oakley

2. Costa Del Mar

3. Ray-Ban

4. Maui Jim

5. Nike

6. Spy+

7. Gucci

8. Versace

9. Under Armour

Men's Sunglasses – Used:

1. Oakley

2. Maui Jim

3. Ray-Ban

4. Costa Del Mar

5. Gucci

6. Spy+

7. Serengeti

8. Versace

9. Smith

Men's Ties - New:

1. Hermes

2. Lilly Pulitzer

3. Donald J. Trump

4. Vineyard Vines

5. Duchamp

6. Brooks Brothers

7. Jerry Garcia

8. Charvet

Men's Ties – Used:

1. Donald J. Trump

2. Charvet

3. Hermes

4. Vineyard Vines

5. Louis Vuitton

6. Salvatore Ferragamo

7. Ben Silver

8. Charles Tyrwhitt

9. Canali

10. Versace

Men's Wallets – New:

1. Harley-Davidson

2. Coach

3. Bacci

4. Louis Vuitton

5. Michael Kors

6. George

7. Anvil

8. Ralph Lauren

9. Tumi

Men's Wallets – Used:

1. Gucci

2. Fossil

3. Louis Vuitton

4. Coach

5. Harley-Davidson

6. Tumi

7. Bosca

8. Burberry

9. Cartier

Men's Hoodies & Sweatshirts – New:

1. Adidas

2. Supreme

3. Nike

4. Affliction

5. Fear of God

6. Harley-Davidson

7. True Religion

8. Anti-Social Social Club

9. American Fighter

10. VLONE

Men's Hoodies & Sweatshirts – Used:

1. Under Armour

2. Polo Ralph Lauren

3. Nike

4. Supreme

5. Harley-Davidson

6. The North Face

7. Adidas

8. Champion

9. BAPE

10. Carhartt

Men's Coats & Jackets – New:

1. Patagonia

2. Arc'teryx

3. Adidas

4. Paradox

5. The North Face

6. Marmot

7. Harley-Davidson

8. Ralph Lauren

Men's Coast & Jackets – Used:

1. Patagonia

2. Harley-Davidson

3. Levi's

4. Arc'teryx

5. The North Face

6. Polo Ralph Lauren

7. Carhartt

8. Schott

9. Marmot

10. Mountain Hardware

Men's Jeans - New:

1. Lucky Brand

2. Rock Revival

3. Bonobos

4. PacSun

5. Kosmo Lupo

6. American Eagle Outfitters

7. Buckle

8. True Religion

9. Versace

10. Calvin Klein

Men's Jeans – Used:

1. Rock Revival

2. Buckle

3. Cinch

4. Levi's

5. Lucky Brand

6. Carhartt

7. American Eagle Outfitters

8. True Religion

9. 7 For All Mankind

10. AG Adriano Goldschmied

Men's Pants - New:

1. Adidas

2. Kuhl

3. Southpole

4. Unionbay

5. EPTM

6. J. Crew

7. Banana Republic

8. Nike

9. Polo Ralph Lauren

Men's Pants – Used:

1. Kuhl

2. Cintas

3. Carhartt

4. 5.11 Tactical

5. Columbia

6. Nike Golf

7. The North Face

8. Bonobos

9. Under Armour

10. J. Crew

Men's Casual Shirts – New:

1. Burberry

2. New Balance

3. Travis Mathew

4. Doublju

5. Tommy Bahama

6. Donald Ross

7. Peter Miller

8. Under Armour

9. Polo Ralph Lauren

10. Vineyard Vines

Men's Casual Button-Down Shirts – Used:

1. Travis Mathew

2. UNTUCKit

3. Lacoste

4. Under Armour

5. Vineyard Vines

6. Kuhl

7. Patagonia

8. Harley-Davidson

9. Southern Tide

10. Reyn Spooner

Men's Dress Shirts – New:

1. Doublju

2. Affliction

3. Jos. A. Bank

4. Charles Tyrwhitt

5. Express

6. Burberry

7. Adidas

8. Hugo Boss

9. Lacoste

10. Ted Baker

Men's Dress Shirts – Used:

1. Brooks Brothers

2. David Donahue

3. Thomas Pink

4. Vineyard Vines

5. Charles Tyrwhitt

6. Turnbull & Asser

7. Lacoste

8. Ralph Lauren Purple Label

9. Brioni

10. Ledbury

Men's T-Shirts – New:

1. American Fighter

2. Armani Exchange

3. Affliction

4. Adidas

5. True Religion

6. Ralph Lauren

7. Harley-Davidson

8. Tommy Bahama

9. Versace

10. Polo Ralph Lauren

Men's T-Shirts – Used:

1. Vineyard Vines

2. Nike

3. Tommy Bahama

4. Harley-Davidson

5. Affliction

6. Under Armour

7. Supreme

8. Polo Ralph Lauren

9. Patagonia

10. Lacoste

Men's Shorts – New:

1. Adidas

2. Diamond Supply Co.

3. Nike Golf

4. Kuhl

5. American Eagle Outfitters

6. True Religion

7. Vineyard Vines

8. Wrangler

9. Mitchell & Ness

Men's Shorts – Used:

1. Nike Golf

2. Columbia

3. Vineyard Vines

4. Patagonia

5. Under Armour

6. The North Face

7. Levi's

8. Polo Ralph Lauren

9. Carhartt

10. Kuhl

Men's Socks - New:

1. Gucci

2. HUF

3. Snap-on

4. PUMA

5. Supreme

6. Ralph Lauren

7. SmartWool

8. Nike

9. Army

10. AND1

Men's Suits & Suit Separates – New:

1. Suit Supply

2. Calvin Klein

3. Lauren Ralph Lauren

4. Tiglio

5. Tommy Hilfiger

6. Alfani

7. Bar III

8. Ryan Seacrest

Men's Suits & Suit Separates – Used:

1. Brooks Brothers

2. Ermenegildo Zegna

3. Jos. A. Bank

4. Hugo Boss

5. J. Crew

6. Banana Republic

7. Canali

8. Suitsupply

9. Armani Collezioni

10. Hickey Freeman

Men's Sweaters – New:

1. Cypress Links

2. Vineyard Vines

3. Peter Millar

4. Tommy Bahama

5. Polo Ralph Lauren

6. Tommy Hilfiger

7. Brooks Brothers

8. J. Crew

9. RRL

Men's Sweaters – Used:

1. Vineyard Vines

2. COOGI

3. Peter Millar

4. Patagonia

5. Kuhl

6. Lacoste

7. Dale of Norway

8. Burberry

9. Nike

10. Brooks Brothers

Men's Swimwear – New:

1. Gucci

2. Burberry

3. Orlebar Brown

4. Vineyard Vines

5. Op

6. Corona

7. Andrew Christian

8. Versace

Men's Swimwear – Used:

1. Patagonia

2. Vineyard Vines

3. Hurley

4. Polo Ralph Lauren

5. Billabong

6. Fox

7. RVCA

8. Oakley

9. Chubbies

Men's Underwear – New ONLY:

1. Tommy John

2. Andrew Christian

3. Duluth Pack

4. Supreme

5. Versace

6. Calvin Klein

7. EQUIPO

8. Tommy Hilfiger

9. Abercrombie & Fitch

10. SAXX

Men's Athletic Shoes – New:

1. Adidas

2. Jordan

3. Hoka One One

4. Nike

5. VANS

6. Salomon

7. Kirkland Signature

8. Cactus

9. Balenciaga

10. Converse

Men's Athletic Shoes – Used:

1. Hoka One One

2. Nike

3. Merrell

4. Jordan

5. Brooks

6. Vibram

7. Adidas

8. Altra

9. New Balance

10. ASICS

Men's Boots – New:

1. PUMA

2. Eddie Bauer

3. Nike

4. Khombu

5. Red Wing Shoes

6. Under Armour

7. Justin Boots

8. Grubs

9. KEEN

10. Chinook

Men's Boots – Used:

1. Red Wing Shoes

2. KEEN

3. Merrell

4. Danner

5. Ariat

6. Harley-Davidson

7. Allen Edmonds

8. Lucchese

9. Timberland

10. Corcoran

Men's Casual Shoes – New:

1. Alpine Swiss

2. PUMA

3. Tom's

4. Sperry Top-Sider

5. Converse

6. Crocs

7. Faded Glory

8. Gucci

9. Sebago

Men's Casual Shoes – Used:

1. Sperry Top-Sider

2. SAS

3. Merrell

4. Gucci

5. Crocs

6. OluKai

7. Cole Haan

8. KEEN

9. ECCO

10. Sanuk

Men's Dress Shoes – New:

1. Dockers

2. Salvatore Ferragamo

3. Gucci

4. Gordon Rush

5. To Boot New York

6. Allen Edmonds

7. Johnston & Murphy

8. Bruno Magli

Men's Dress Shoes – Used:

1. Allen Edmonds

2. Gucci

3. Salvatore Ferragamo

4. Alden

5. Cole Haan

6. Magnanni

7. Bally

8. Bruno Magli

9. Brooks Brothers

10. Ferragamo

Men's Sandals – New:

1. Oakley

2. Nike

3. Rainbow

4. Supreme

5. Khombu

6. KEEN

7. OluKai

8. Adidas

9. Under Armour

10. Jordan

Men's Sandals – Used:

1. Chaco

2. KEEN

3. Birkenstock

4. Nike

5. Crocs

6. Teva

7. OluKai

8. Reef

9. Gucci

10. Adidas

Women's Belts – New:

1. Kate Spade New York

2. G.I.L.I.

3. Michael Kors

4. Tory Burch

5. Burberry

6. Gucci

7. Calvin Klein

8. Fossil

9. Salvatore Ferragamo

10. Anthropologie

Women's Belts – Used:

1. Gucci

2. Hermes

3. Coach

4. Chanel

5. Tony Lama

6. Lucky Brand

7. Linea Pelle

8. Michael Kors

9. CAbi

10. Chico's

Women's Hair Accessories – New:

1. Chanel

2. Lilla Rose

3. Lululemon

4. Hair Glove

5. Lilly Pulitzer

6. Missoni

7. Nike

8. Natural Life

9. France Luxe

10. Anthropologie

Women's' Handbag Accessories by Type:

1. Dust Covers

2. Tags/Fobs

3. Charms

4. Organizers

5. Locks

6. Makeup Bags

7. Hard Cases

8. Straps/Handles

9. Keychains

10. Shells

Women's Handbag Accessories - New:

1. Kate Spade New York

2. Louis Vuitton

3. Gucci

4. Thirty-One

5. Vera Bradley

6. Michael Kors

7. Chanel

8. Dooney & Bourke

9. Longchamp

10. Chloe

Women's Handbag Accessories – Used:

1. Gucci

2. Chanel

3. Louis Vuitton

4. Kate Spade New York

5. Michael Kors

6. Dooney & Bourke

7. Coach

8. Hermes

9. Fossil

10. Miche

Women's Hats – New:

1. Harley-Davidson

2. Judith March

3. J. Crew

4. Helen Kaminski

5. Nike

6. Adidas

7. Lululemon

8. Victoria's Secret

9. Bebe

Women's Hats – Used:

1. Helen Kaminski

2. Eric Javits

3. Scala

4. Burberry

5. Lululemon

6. Coach

7. Harley-Davidson

8. Betmar

9. Moncler

Women's Scarves & Wraps – New:

1. Kate Spade

2. Burberry

3. Fendi

4. Hermes

5. Chan Luu

6. Louis Vuitton

7. Eileen Fisher

8. LuLaRoe

9. Talbots

10. Alexander McQueen

Women's Scarves & Wraps – Used:

1. Coach

2. Louis Vuitton

3. Burberry

4. Hermes

5. Lilly Pulitzer

6. Liberty of London

7. Gucci

8. Talbots

9. Ralph Lauren

10. Lululemon

Women's Sunglasses – New:

1. Oakley

2. Brighton

3. Ray-Ban

4. Gucci

5. Maui Jim

6. Jessica Simpson

7. Costa Del Mar

8. Tiffany & Co.

9. Michael Kors

10. Polo Ralph Lauren

Women's Sunglasses – Used:

1. Oakley

2. Coach

3. Ray-Ban

4. Prada

5. Chanel

6. Versace

7. Kate Spade New York

8. Maui Jim

9. Gucci

10. Brighton

Women's Wallets – New:

1. Kate Spade New York

2. Michael Kors

3. Vera Bradley

4. Hobo International

5. Coach

6. Brahmin

7. Patricia Nash

8. Thirty-One

9. Louis Vuitton

10. Tory Burch

Women's Wallets – Used:

1. Kate Spade New York

2. Coach

3. Michael Kors

4. Fossil

5. Dooney & Bourke

6. Hobo International

7. Louis Vuitton

8. Tory Burch

9. Brahmin

10. Vera Bradley

Women's Hoodies & Sweatshirts – New:

1. Affliction

2. Adidas

3. Victoria's Secret

4. Juicy Couture

5. PINK

6. Brandy Melville

7. Nike

8. Free People

9. Wildfox

Women's Hoodies & Sweatshirts – Used:

1. Victoria's Secret

2. PINK

3. Lucky Brand

4. Harley-Davidson

5. Vineyard Vines

6. Under Armour

7. Nike

8. Juicy Couture

9. Wildfox

10. Adidas

Women's Coats, Jackets & Vests – New:

1. Joseph Ribkoff

2. Hunter

3. Patagonia

4. LuLaRoe

5. Johnny Was

6. 32 Degrees

7. Doublju

8. Eileen Fisher

9. Chico's

10. Zara

Women's Coats, Jackets & Vests – Used:

1. Patagonia

2. Eileen Fisher

3. Harley-Davidson

4. The North Face

5. Marmot

6. Burberry

7. Levi's

8. Torrid

9. Misook

10. Chico's

Women's Dresses – New:

1. LuLaRoe

2. Lilly Pulitzer

3. J. Jill

4. Athleta

5. eShakti

6. Ted Baker

7. Zimmermann

8. Talbots

9. Agnes & Dora

10. Torrid

Women's Dresses – Used:

1. LuLaRoe

2. Athleta

3. Fresh Produce

4. Lilly Pulitzer

5. Torrid

6. J. Jill

7. Patagonia

8. Prana

9. Eileen Fisher

10. Boeden

Women's Bras & Bra Sets – New:

1. Enell

2. Spanx

3. Cacique

4. Wacoal

5. Breezies

6. Olga

7. Victoria's Secret

8. Chantelle

9. Genie Bra

10. Soma Intimates

Women's Bras & Bra Sets – Used:

1. Wacoal

2. Soma Intimates

3. Victoria's Secret

4. Cacique

5. Olga

6. Moving Comfort

7. Chantelle

8. Lilyette

9. Warner's

10. Bali

Women's Panties – New ONLY:

1. Olga

2. Thinx

3. Soma Intimates

4. Cacique

5. Under Armour

6. Jockey

7. Warner's

8. Victoria's Secret

9. Spanx

10. Lane Bryant

Women's Shapewear – New:

1. Spanx

2. Miss Belt

3. Tecnomed

4. Donna Karen

5. Naomi & Nicole

6. Marilyn Monroe

7. Belly Bandit

8. Kymaro

9. Cacique

10. Slim N Lift

Women's Shapewear – Used:

1. Spanx

2. Flexees

3. Maidenform

4. Bali

5. Ardyss

6. Nancy Ganz

7. Miraclesuit

8. Yummie Tummie

Women's Sleepwear & Robes – New:

1. Eileen West

2. Croft & Barrow

3. Secret Treasures

4. In Bloom by Jonquil

5. Miss Elaine

6. J. Crew

7. Lauren Ralph Lauren

8. Victoria's Secret

9. Carole Hochman

10. Gilligan & O'Malley

Women's Sleepwear & Robes – Used:

1. Eileen West

2. Lauren Ralph Lauren

3. Natori

4. Victoria's Secret

5. Miss Elaine

6. Nick & Nora

7. Vanity Fair

8. Soma Intimates

9. Carole Hochman

10. Lilly Pulitzer

Women's Jeans – New:

1. Madewell

2. American Eagle Outfitters

3. FRAME

4. Torrid

5. Gloria Vanderbilt

6. Citizens of Humanity

7. Earl Jean

8. Jessica Simpson

9. Lane Bryant

10. Maurices

Women's Jeans – Used:

1. Rock Revival

2. Mother

3. Rag & Bone

4. Miss Me

5. Torris

6. NYDJ

7. American Eagle Outfitters

8. Madewell

9. Lane Bryant

10. Wrangler

Women's Jumpsuits & Rompers – New:

1. Lilly Pulitzer

2. Cabi

3. Old Navy

4. Gap

5. Anthropologie

6. Free People

7. Torrid

8. Banana Republic

9. Vince Camuto

10. Madewell

Women's Jumpsuits & Rompers – Used:

1. Lilly Pulitzer

2. Free People

3. Madewell

4. Old Navy

5. Anthropologie

6. Zara

7. Gap

8. Ann Taylor

9. Bebe

10. J. Crew

Women's Leggings – New:

1. LuLaRoe

2. ALO

3. Lilly Pulitzer

4. Spanx

5. Felina

6. Faded Glory

7. Torrid

8. Victoria's Secret

9. Adidas

10. Lululemon

Women's Leggings – Used:

1. Victoria's Secret

2. LuLaRoe

3. PINK

4. Spanx

5. Lysse

6. Lululemon

7. HUE

8. Cabi

9. Black Milk

10. Torrid

Women's Pants – New:

1. Adidas

2. Chico's

3. Eileen Fisher

4. Women with Control

5. J. Jill

6. Quacker Factory

7. Athleta

8. Denim & Co.

9. Joseph Ribkoff

10. FLAX

Women's Pants – Used:

1. Eileen Fisher

2. FLAX

3. Chico's

4. Kuhl

5. Prana

6. J. Jill

7. Columbia

8. REI

9. Lululemon

10. Soft Surroundings

Women's Shorts – New:

1. Lilly Pulitzer

2. American Eagle Outfitters

3. Torrid

4. Madewell

5. Bandolino

6. J. Crew

7. Karen Scott

8. Diane Gilman

9. Chico's

10. Victoria's Secret

Women's Shorts – Used:

1. Miss Me

2. American Eagle Outfitters

3. Lilly Pulitzer

4. Torrid

5. Buckle

6. Patagonia

7. Vineyard Vines

8. Hudson

9. Lucky Brand

10. Columbia

Women's Suits & Suit Separates – New:

1. Veronica Beard

2. J. Crew

3. Ashro

4. Nicole Miller

5. Express

6. H&M

7. Banana Republic

8. White House Black Market

9. Theory

10. St. John

Women's Suits & Suit Separates – Used:

1. St. John

2. Torrid

3. Theory

4. J. Crew

5. Eileen Fisher

6. White House Black Market

7. Tahari

8. Le Suit

9. Brooks Brothers

10. Zara

Women's Sweaters – New:

1. Storybook Knits

2. LuLaRoe

3. J. Crew

4. Eileen Fisher

5. Talbots

6. Lilly Pulitzer

7. Free People

8. White House Black Market

9. Cabi

10. Chico's

Women's Sweaters – Used:

1. Eileen Fisher

2. LuLaRoe

3. Lilly Pulitzer

4. Misook

5. J. Crew

6. Vince

7. J. Jill

8. Theory

9. Tory Burch

10. St. John

Women's Swimwear – New:

1. Athleta

2. Lane Bryant

3. Land's End

4. Catalina

5. J. Crew

6. Torrid

7. Cacique

8. Ava & Viv

9. Miraclesuit

10. Victoria's Secret

Women's Swimsuits – Used:

1. Miraclesuit

2. Lands' End

3. Athleta

4. Victoria's Secret

5. Maxine of Hollywood

6. Longitude

7. Speedo

8. Jantzen

9. J. Crew

10. Catalina

Women's Tops – New:

1. Simply Southern
2. LuLaRoe
3. Lilly Pulitzer
4. Affliction
5. Adidas
6. J. Jill
7. American Fighter
8. Torrid
9. Johnny Was
10. Catherine's

Women's Tops – Used:

1. Eileen Fisher
2. Torrid
3. FLAX
4. J. Jill
5. Johnny Was
6. Lilly Pulitzer

7. Catherine's

8. Soft Surroundings

9. LOGO by Lori Goldstein

10. Simply Southern

Women's Athletic Shoes – New:

1. Adidas

2. Balenciaga

3. Hoka One One

4. Michael Kors

5. Converse

6. Nike

7. Zumba

8. Coach

9. Jordan

10. VANS

Women's Athletic Shoes – Used:

1. Brooks

2. Hoka One One

3. Converse

4. Nike

5. Skechers

6. ASICS

7. Vibram

8. Altra

9. Merrell

10. Adidas

Women's Boots – New:

1. Freebird By Steven

2. Henry Ferrera

3. Hunter

4. Torrid

5. Tory Burch

6. Merona

7. Red Wing Shoes

8. Harley-Davidson

9. Justin Boots

10. Burberry

Women's Boots – Used:

1. Ariat

2. Harley-Davidson

3. Dr. Martens

4. Hunter

5. Justin Boots

6. Frye

7. Lucchese

8. Merrell

9. KEEN

10. Corral Boots

Women's Flats – New:

1. Tom's

2. Tory Burch

3. Michael Kors

4. Coach

5. PUMA

6. Gucci

7. Dr. Scholl's

8. JBU

9. Sperry Top-Sider

10. J. Crew

Women's Flats – Used:

1. Tieks

2. Tom's

3. Tory Burch

4. Alegria

5. Crocs

6. KEEN

7. J. Crew

8. Vionic

9. Coach

10. Birkenstock

Women's Heels – New:

1. Diesel

2. Lotta from Stockholm

3. Tory Burch

4. Michael Kors

5. Ann Taylor

6. Charlotte Olympia

7. Christian Louboutin

8. Kate Spade New York

9. Coach

10. Jack Rogers

Women's Heels – Used:

1. Tom's

2. Tory Burch

3. Christian Louboutin

4. Michaels Kors

5. Crocs

6. Kate Spade New York

7. Dansko

8. Manolo Blahnik

9. FLY London

10. Coach

Women's Sandals – New:

1. Nike

2. Tory Burch

3. Birchenstock

4. Michael Kors

5. Dawgs

6. Chaco

7. Vionic

8. Gucci

9. Born

10. Teva

Women's Sandals – Used:

1. Birkenstock

2. Chaco

3. KEEN

4. Teva

5. Dansko

6. Tory Burch

7. Clarks

8. Crocs

9. Born

10. Vionic

Luggage – New:

1. Tumi

2. Travelers Club

3. Samsonite

4. Filson

5. TAG

6. RIMOWA

7. Harley-Davidson

8. Goplus

9. Victoria's Secret

10. Vera Bradley

Luggage – Used:

1. Tumi

2. TAG

3. Samsonite

4. Louis Vuitton

5. Briggs & Riley

6. Zero Halliburton

7. Hartmann

8. Brighton

9. DELSEY

10. American Tourister

CHAPTER 6

COLLECTIBLES

Clothing is the largest category on Ebay, and collectibles is the second. Most collectibles don't sell on brand alone but on style, era, and condition combined. That makes narrowing down the best-selling individual collectible brands in each subcategory nearly impossible. Instead, I'm providing you with the best-selling categories of collectibles, along with the top results in five popular categories that are frequently found in thrift stores and at garage sales.

Each of the collectible categories and subcategories could easily fill individual books of their own; if you are interested in a particular topic, say coins or pens, there are dedicated guides both in published books and online that go in-depth on each. Many of these genres also have dedicated Facebook groups that can be a wealth of knowledge. A simple internet or Facebook search of the category you are interested in will bring up dozens of results.

Popular Vintage Collectibles:

- Coins

- Stamps

- Advertising

- Disneyana

- Militaria

- Montblanc Fountain Pens

- Postcards

- Comics

- Arcade, Jukebox & Pinball Machines & Parts

- Radio, Phonograph, TV, and Phone

- Ethnic & Cultural

- Pens & Writing Instruments

- Historical Memorabilia

- Non-Sport Trading Cards

- Star Wars

- Funko

- Knives, Swords & Blades

- Tobacciana

- Sports Cards

- Agriculture

Japanese Anime:

1. UPC Codes

2. Danbo

3. Yo-Kai Watch Medal

4. Tokyo Ghoul Figure

5. Doujinshi

6. Asuna Figure

7. Sonic Plush

8. Gashapon

9. Kuroko No Basuke

10. Anime Cels

11. Gloomy Bear

12. Kamen Rider

13. Myth Cloth

Comic Book Figurines:

1. Thanos

2. Venom

3. Silver Surfer

4. Captain Marvel

5. Gamora

6. X-23

7. Supergirl

8. Punisher

9. Wonder Woman

10. Red Skull

Graphic Novels:

1. Dr. Strange

2. Titans

3. Watchmen

4. Sgt. Rock

5. Sonic the Hedgehog

6. Captain Marvel

7. Warlock

8. Silver Surfer

9. Sandman

10. Batman

Trading Card Singles:

1. Pop Century

2. Ghostbusters

3. Marvel Premier

4. Lost in Space

5. Firefly

6. Twilight Zone

7. Planet of the Apes

8. Ninja Turtles

9. Three Stooges

10. The Walking Dead

Funko Pop:

1. Deadpool

2. Vinyl Box Protectors

3. Exclusive (Target, Walmart, The Limited, Hot Topic)

4. Metallic

5. Spiderman

6. Cull Obsidian

7. Wacky Wobbler

8. Venom

9. Chase

10. Conan

11. Star Wars

12. Kidrobot

13. DC Comics

14. Marvel

Crystals:

1. Bismuth Crystals

2. Unopened Geodes

3. Madagascar Banded Agate

4. Chrysocolla

5. Polished Stones

6. Glass Balls

7. Crystal Clusters

8. Palm Stone

9. Shiva Lingam

10. Black Tourmaline

11. Selenite

12. Chrysocolla Rough

13. Herkimer Diamond

14. Aura Quartz

15. Selenite

CHAPTER 7

ELECTRONICS

To be honest, I almost left electronics out of this book. Just like with cameras, the sheer number of models makes providing the best-selling brands difficult. Electronics are also a more specialized category than, say, clothing. It's relatively easy to spot a decent pair of sneakers; but figuring out the difference between a subwoofer and a power inverter takes more skill.

Therefore, rather than brands, this chapter features the TYPES of items that sell best. I use these lists to help me when I'm looking through estate sale ads as secondhand and vintage electronics can actually bring in more money than new ones. If I see that printers are advertised, for instance, I'll then do a quick search of the brands they've listed to see if they'll be worth picking up to sell on Ebay.

Most buyers also expect electronics to be fully tested. Testing electronics is not a skill I possess, nor one I'm interested in learning. If you do pick up electronics and are unable to test them, you will likely have to list them for parts.

Computers, Printers and Parts:

- 3D Printers & Supplies

- Cables & Connectors

- Computer Components & Parts

- Desktops

- Drives, Storage & Blank Media

- Servers

- Networking

- Keyboards, Mice & Pointers

- Laptops

- Monitors & Projectors

- Power Protection

- Printers, Scanners & Supplies

- Software

- Tablets & eBook Readers

Consumer Electronics

- Home Telephones & Accessories – Cordless Telephones & Handsets

- Battery Chargers

- Rechargeable Batteries

- Single Use Batteries

- Portable Audio & Headphones – Audio Docks & Mini Speakers, iPods & MP3 Players

- Walkie Talkies

- Two-Way Radios

- Home Surveillance

- Home Audio

- Media Streamers

- DVD & Blu-ray Players

- Home Theatre Projectors

- Audio Cables & Interconnects

- Remote Controls

- Record Players

- TV Boards, Parts & Components

Vehicle Electronics:

- Car Amplifiers

- Car Audio In-Dash Units

- Car Speakers & Speaker Systems

- Car Subwoofers

- Power Inverters

- Rear View Monitors/Cameras & Kits

- Video In-Dash Units w/ GPS

- GPS Units

- Marine Audio

- Radar & Laser Detectors

Vintage Electronics:

- Reel-To-Reel Tape Recorders

- Amplifiers & Tube Amps

- Tubes & Tube Sockets

- Record Players

- Speakers

- Stereo Receivers

CHAPTER 8

CRAFTS:

Craft supplies are found at nearly ever garage sale in my area. While most aren't worth anything on Ebay, there are certain items that are highly sought after. Vintage markers are especially hot (make sure they still work); and large lots of beads, fabric and yarn sell well. Scrapbooking is no longer the hot category it once was, but acrylic stamps still have a market for those who journal and make cards. Usually when I sell craft supplies, I sell them in lots of mixed brands, such as 50 packages of stickers or 100 rolls of ribbon.

Art Pens & Markers:

1. Tombow

2. 3Doodler

3. Sharpie

4. Copic

5. Micron

6. Zebra

7. Faber-Castell

8. Prismacolor

9. STABILO

10. Chameleon

Beads: lots of 1000

- Glass

- Mixed Metals

- Metal

- Seed

- Wood

- Stone

- Acrylic

- Gold

Fabric: Licensed character fabric, such as Disney or Peanuts, is highly sought after by crafters. You likely won't be able to find brand names on secondhand fabric; instead, so look for great prints and a large amount. Crafters turn to Ebay to buy fabric in bulk.

Yarn: Yarn is best sold in lots on Ebay. I stick to yarn that is still new in the package and that I have several skeins of in the same color.

Leather Stamping: Vintage leather stamping kits can be extremely valuable.

Scrapbook Die Cut & Embossing Machines

1. Cricut

2. Gina

3. Silhouette

4. Anna Griffin

5. Heartfelt Creations

6. Crafter's Companion

7. Stampin' Up

8. Brother

9. Lace

10. Cross

11. Sizzix

12. QuicKutz

13. Cuttlebug

14. Ellison

Sewing Machines:

1. Singer

2. Toyota

3. Brother

4. Michley

5. Husqvarna Viking

6. Bernina

7. PFAFF

8. Janome

9. Baby Lock

10. Kenmore

Acrylic Stamps:

1. Stampin' Up

2. Stampa Rosa

3. House-Mouse

4. My Favorite Things

CHAPTER 9

HEALTH & BEAUTY

Unless it is vintage, Ebay prohibits the sale of used cosmetics. Makeup and skin care are great items to pick up in the clearance aisles of retail stores or through liquidation companies. Be sure to double check expiration dates. While some items will still sell once they've expired, fresh items bring in more money.

Note that liquids and flammable materials, such as the alcohol used in perfumes, can only be sent via ground mail, i.e. NOT through the Post Office via First Class or Priority. Some international countries also prohibit cosmetics to be shipped to their residents. If you ship through Ebay's Global Shipping program, you'll be alerted immediately if a country blocks the sale of an item you are listing so that you can just remove them from the shipping options.

Body Lotions & Moisturizers:

1. Bath & Body Works

2. Victoria's Secret

3. Philosophy

4. Estee Lauder

5. Lancome

6. Dior

7. Burberry

8. Chanel

9. Coach

10. The Body Shop

Men's Fragrances:

1. Chanel

2. Jafra

3. Abercrombie & Fitch

4. Avon

5. Creed

6. Giorgio Armani

7. Mary Kay

8. Coach

9. Calvin Klein

10. Dior

Unisex Fragrances:

1. Kenneth Cole

2. Maison Francis Kurkdjian

3. Pure Romance

4. Calvin Klein

5. Frederic Malle

6. Diptyque

7. Kilian

8. Byredo

9. Aveda

10. Salvatore Ferragamo

Women's Fragrances:

1. Chanel

2. T.O.V.A.

3. Avon

4. Halle Berry

5. Mary Kay

6. Pacifica

7. BeautiControl

8. JAFRA

9. Nest Fragrances

10. Victoria's Secret

Hair Color:

1. Olaplex

2. Vidal Sassoon

3. Aveda

4. Liese

5. John Frieda

6. Youthair

7. Everpro

8. Tressa

9. Color Wow

10. Sun-In

Hair Dyes:

1. Dyson

2. T3

3. DevaCurl

4. Xtava

5. Drybar

6. Parlux

7. BaByliss PRO

8. InStyler

9. Revlon

10. Solano

Hair Loss Treatments:

1. NUTRAFOL

2. ROGAINE

3. Caboki

4. Shapiro MD

5. Viviscal

6. Monat

7. Keranique

8. iGrow

9. Rite Aid

10. Qilib

Relaxers & Straightening Products:

1. Cadiveu Professional

2. Keratin Complex

3. Brazilian Blowout

4. Bio Iconic

5. Acai

6. Pura d'or

7. Enjoy

8. Ahglow

9. Shiseido

10. Alfaparf Milano

Shampoos & Conditioners:

1. Lush

2. Nizoral

3. Monat

4. WEN

5. Silk18

6. Just for Men

7. Pureology

8. Kevin Murphy

9. Aveda

10. Art Naturals

Straightening & Curing Irons:

1. InStyler

2. Tyme

3. T3

4. CHI

5. BaByliss PRO

6. DAFNI

7. Sarah Potempa

8. Cartier

9. Ghd

10. Royale

Styling Products:

1. Focus 21

2. Layrite

3. Samy

4. Avenda

5. Kevin Murphy

6. WEN

7. Suavecito

8. Drybar

9. Nick Chavez

10. Lush

Treatments, Oils & Protectors:

1. Monat

2. Moroccanoil

3. HerStyler

4. BioSilk

5. Aussie

6. Ojon

7. Global Keratin

8. Olaplex

9. Paul Mitchel

10. Loanza

Glucose Test Strips:

1. Freestyle

2. OneTouch

3. Precision Xtra

4. Breeze 2

5. Abbott

6. Contour

7. T.R.U.E. TEST

8. Rugby

9. Accu-Chek

10. ReliOn

Over-the-Counter Medicines for Digestion & Nausea:

1. Align

2. Nexium

3. Zegerid

4. Prilosec OTC

5. CVS

6. DUO

7. Prevacid

8. Ultra

9. Equate

10. Bayer

Pain & Fever Relief:

1. Voltaren

2. Nurofen

3. Myoflex

4. Schiff

5. Australian Dream

6. COLD-FX

7. Omron

8. Natureplex

9. Neuragen

10. Biofreeze

Eye Shadow:

1. Anastasia Beverly Hills

2. Huda Beauty

3. Anastasia

4. Too Faced

5. Morpe

6. Younique

7. Tarte

8. Kat Von D

9. Urban Decay

10. Mary Kay

Eyeliner:

1. Kat Von D

2. Mary Kay

3. MAC

4. Marc Jacobs

5. Almay

6. Tarte

7. IT Cosmetics

8. Chanel

9. Origins

10. Avon

False Eyelashes:

1. Diva

2. Revlon

3. Sephora

4. Orly

5. Huda Beauty

6. Duo

7. Perfect

8. House of Lashes

9. Diamond

10. Velour Lashes

Mascara:

1. Younique

2. Mary Kay

3. Too Faced

4. Benefit

5. IT Cosmetics

6. Tarte

7. Urban Decay

8. Lancome

9. Chanel

10. Eyeko

Face Powder:

1. Laura Mercier

2. Mary Kay

3. Rodan + Fields

4. IT Cosmetics

5. WUNDER2

6. Secret

7. Coty

8. Lancome

9. BeautiControl

10. Hourglass

Foundation:

1. IT Cosmetics

2. Mary Kay

3. Merle Norman

4. Younique

5. Sheer Cover

6. Dermacol

7. BeautiControl

8. Luminess Air

9. Urban Decay

10. Chanel

Lipstick:

1. LipSense

2. Huda Beauty

3. Younique

4. Kylie

5. IT Cosmetics

6. Mary Kay

7. Charlotte Tilbury

8. Aveda

9. Crème

10. Chanel

Makeup Bags & Cases - New:

1. Chanel

2. Vera Bradley

3. Kate Spade New York

4. Orla Kiely

5. Burberry

6. Mary Kay

7. MAC

8. Annie

9. Thirty-One

10. Prada

Makeup Bags & Cases – Used:

1. Vera Bradley

2. Kate Spade New York

3. Caboodles

4. Thirty-One

5. Chanel

6. Fossil

7. Mary Kay

8. Tory Burch

9. Coach

10. Louis Vuitton

Makeup Brushes:

1. IT Cosmetics

2. LA MER

3. Marc Jacobs

4. Tarte

5. Kat Von D

6. Bobbi Brown

7. Younique

8. Mary Kay

9. Hourglass

10. Too Faced

Medical & Mobility:

- Hearing Assistance (hearing aids and batteries)

- Incontinence Aids (adult pads and diapers)

- Wheelchairs & Replacement Parts

- Orthotics, Braces & Sleeves

Gel Nails (polish, kits, and systems):

1. Jamberry

2. Gelish

3. SensatioNail

4. CND

5. OPI

6. Elite99

7. Young Nails

8. Nailene

9. Hard & Nail Harmony

10. Light Elegance

Nail Art Accessories (sheets, kits, sets, and accents):

1. Jamberry

2. Nailene

3. Mia Secret

4. Cuccio

5. Nabi

6. Sally Hansen

7. BMC

8. Young Nails

9. Nicole

10. OPI

Nail Polish:

1. Incoco

2. Dermelect

3. Amazing Shine

4. Chanel

5. Jamberry

6. Masglo

7. Christian Louboutin

8. Del Sol

9. OPI

10. Illamasqua

Aromatheraphy:

1. Naked

2. PAX

3. Cuttwood

4. One Hit Wonder

5. Cloud

6. Candy

7. Young Living

8. doTERRA

9. MONQ

10. Eden's Garden

11. 21 Drops

Electric Toothbrushes (including replacement handles and chargers:

1. Philips Sonicare

2. Oral-B

3. Waterpik

4. FOREO

5. Sonic

6. Brush Buddies

7. Rotadent

8. CVS

9. Arm & Hammer

10. Colgate

Hair Clippers & Trimmers:

1. Wahl

2. Remington

3. Andis

4. BaByliss PRO

5. Flowbee

6. BaByliss

7. Philips Norelco

8. Conair

9. Panasonic

10. Kemei

Men's Electric Shavers:

1. Philips Norelco

2. Braun

3. Wahl

4. Andis

5. Remington

6. Mangroomer

7. Philips

8. Skull Shaver

9. Panasonic

10. Kemei

Laser Hair Removal:

1. Braun

2. Remington

3. Silk

4. Gillette

5. Tria

6. Tanda

7. Iluminage

8. LumaRX

9. Syneron

10. Candela

Men's Razon Blades:

1. Gillette

2. Astra

3. Schick

4. Personna

5. Feather

6. TORQ

7. Shark

8. Dorco

9. Panasonic

10. Lord

Acne & Blemish Treatments:

1. Rodan + Fields

2. Proactiv

3. Mary Kay

4. Exposed Skin Care

5. Origins

6. Dr. Brandt Skin Care

7. Galderma

8. Murad

9. BeautiControl

10. Cellusyn

Anti-Aging Products:

1. Nerium

2. Rodan + Fields

3. Arbonne

4. Mary Kay

5. Boots No. 7

6. Jeunesse

7. Drunk Elephant

8. Derm Exclusive

9. Avon

Cleansers & Toners:

1. Mary Kay

2. Origins

3. COSRX

4. Lush

5. SkinMedica

6. BeautiControl

7. Fresh

8. Mario Badescu

9. Jan Marini

10. Proactiv

Eye Treatments & Masks:

1. Mary Kay

2. LA MER

3. Kiehl's

4. Benefit

5. Avon

6. Revision

7. Mizon

8. Laneige

9. TATCHA

10. Chamonix

Home Skin Care Devices:

1. Microcurrent Therapy

2. Electric Facial Brush

3. Replacement Tips & Wands

4. Seals

5. Brushes

6. Facial Brushes

7. Cleansers

8. Face Life Macine

9. Nib

10. Replacement Brush/Head

Home Skin Care Device Brands:

1. NuFACE

2. FOREO

3. Clarisonic

4. Vanity Planet

5. Olay

6. Clinique

7. Silk

8. Nuskin

9. Michael Todd

10. JeNu

Lightening Creams:

1. Proactiv

2. Golden Pearl

3. Bio Claire

4. Caro White

5. Fashion Fair

6. Nuskin

7. Nadinola

8. Image

9. AMBI

10. Xtreme Brite

Masks & Peels:

1. My Beauty Diary

2. Aztec Secret

3. Baby Foot

4. SkinMedica

5. Ole Hanriksen

6. Kiehl's

7. Laneige

8. Cle de Peau Beaute

9. Chanel

10. SHILLS

Moisturizers:

1. Melaleuca

2. Mary Kay

3. LA MER

4. Josie Maran

5. BeautiControl

6. TATCHA

7. Lush

8. Origins

9. Avon

10. Charlotte Tilbury

Sunscreen:

1. Biore

2. Vanicream

3. Rodan + Fields

4. Rohto

5. La Roche-Posay

6. TIZO

7. Supergoop!

8. Kiehl's

9. The Face Shop

10. EltaMD

Eyeglass Frames - New:

1. Oakley

2. Ray-Ban

3. Cartier

4. Gucci

5. Tiffany & Co.

6. Versace

7. Chanel

8. Miraflex

9. TAG Heuer

10. Oliver Peoples

Eyeglass Frames – Used:

1. Oakley

2. Ray-Ban

3. Warby Parker

4. Chanel

5. Versace

6. Persol

7. PRADA

8. Silhouette

9. Tiffany & Co.

10. Gucci

Reading Glasses:

1. Swarovski

2. Cheetah

3. Betsey Johnson

4. CliC

5. ThinOPTICS

6. Joy

7. Miasto Eyewear

8. Foster Grant

9. ISU Eyewear

10. Eyebobs

Energy Bars, Drinks & Pills:

1. Advocare

2. Arbonne

3. Shakeology

4. Beachbody

5. It Works!

6. Organifi

7. Zurvita

8. Zija

9. Zeal for Life

10. Yoli

Herbs & Botanicals:

1. Shaklee

2. XANGO

3. Swanson Health Products

4. Sprout Everything SuperFoods

5. Atomy

6. MuscleTech

7. Pfizer

8. Organo Gold

9. Vital Nutrients

10. Thorne Research

Vitamins & Minerals:

1. Prevagen

2. Standard Process

3. Instaflex

4. NUTRILITE

5. Onnit

6. Swanson Health Products

7. Nordic Naturals

8. Alli

9. Juice Plus+

10. OMEGA

Detox & Cleansers:

1. Plexus

2. Isagenix

3. It Works!

4. Advocare

5. Arbonne

6. Total Life Changes

7. Zija

8. Beachbody

9. ASEA

10. MonaVie

Meal Replacement Drinks:

1. Plexus

2. Isagenix

3. Garden of Life

4. Optifast

5. Visalus

6. Arbonne

7. Herbalife

8. Slim Fast

9. Shakeology

10. 310 Nutrition

Weight Loss Program Foods:

1. Ideal Protein

2. Medifast

3. Isagenix

4. Nutrisystem

5. South Beach Diet

6. Quest Nutrition

7. Atkins

8. IdealShape

9. 4Life

10. HMR

CHAPTER 10

HOME & GARDEN:

I go to a lot of estate sales in search of items to sell on Ebay, so I spend quite a bit of time listing in the Home & Garden categories! My favorite items to sell are lots of vintage flatware, which crafters bend to make jewelry. I also look for new-in-package kitchen items and replacement parts.

Coffee Pods:

1. Tassimo

2. Flavia

3. Nespresso

4. Gevalia

5. Starbucks

6. San Francisco Bay

7. Kirkland Signature

8. Grove Square

9. Maxwell House

10. Dunkin' Donuts

Tea:

1. Starbucks

2. ORIHIRO

3. Teavana

4. Paradise

5. ITO EN

6. Taylor

7. Homemade

8. PG Tips

9. Bigelow

10. Traditional Medicinals

Candles:

1. Diptyque

2. Luminara

3. Aveda

4. Bath & Body Works

5. Yankee Candle

6. Henri Bendel

7. VOLUSPA

8. Scentsy

9. Jo Malone

10. Scentsational Soaps & Candles

Air Fresheners:

1. Poo-Pourri

2. Ozium

3. Bath & Body Works

4. Glade

5. Claire Burke

6. Little Trees

7. Yankee Candle

8. Chemical Guys

9. Scentsy

10. Crabtree & Evelyn

Steak Knives - New:

1. Cutco

2. WUSTHOF

3. Miracle Blade

4. Case

5. Pampered Chef

6. Shun

7. Ergo Chef

8. Global

9. OXO

10. Old Hickory

Steak Knives – Used:

1. Cutco

2. WUSTHOF

3. Chicago Cutlery

4. Pampered Chef

5. Zwilling J.A. Henckels

6. Shun

7. Gerber

8. Victorinox

9. Laguiole

10. Ronco

Flatware - New:

1. Crown

2. Pottery Barn

3. Jean Dubost

4. Hampton Forge

5. Ralph Lauren

6. Snap-On

7. Cutco

8. Disney

9. Fiesta

10. Waterford

Flatware – Used: Note that large lots of vintage mixed flatware, especially spoons and forks, with decorative handles are especially sought after by crafters who bend them into jewelry.

1. MSI

2. Christofle

3. MONO

4. Oneida

5. Dansk

6. Fiesta

7. Revere

8. Interpur

Pottery & Glass:

1. Rae Dunn

2. Christofle

3. Apilco

4. Hermes

5. Steelite International

6. Swid Powell

7. Anthropologie

8. Varages

9. Mary Kay

10. Emma Bridgewater

Espresso & Cappuccino Machines – New:

1. Breville

2. Nespresso

3. DeLonghi

4. Mr. Coffee

5. Imusa

6. Chemex

7. Bella

8. VonShef

9. Krups

10. Briel

Espresso & Cappuccino Machines – Used:

1. DeLonghi

2. Nespresso

3. Breville

4. Mr. Coffee

5. Saeco

6. Krups

7. FrancisFrancis

8. Starbucks

9. LaPavoni

10. Keurig

Countertop Blenders – New:

1. Ninja

2. Vitamix

3. NutriBullet

4. VonShef

5. Magic Bullet

6. Oster

7. Margaritaville

8. Blendtec

9. Breville

10. Bella Cucina

Countertop Blenders – Used:

1. Vitamix

2. Ninja

3. Margaritaville

4. Blendtec

5. Montel

6. NutriBullet

7. KitchenAid

8. Magic Bullet

9. Waring Pro

10. Cuisinart

Countertop Mixers:

1. KitchenAid

2. Cuisinart

3. Whirlpool

4. Ninja

5. Breville

6. Bosch

7. PLUS

8. Hamilton Beach

9. Klarstein

10. Flex

Countertop Mixers – Used:

1. Bosch

2. Hobart

3. KitchenAid

4. Sunbeam

5. Oster

6. Kenwood

7. Farberware

Juicers – New:

1. Breville

2. Proctor Silex

3. VonShef

4. OMEGA

5. Jack LaLanne

6. BLACK+DECKER

7. Bella

8. KitchenAid

9. Chef'n

10. Hurom

Juicers – Used:

1. Champion

2. OMEGA

3. Breville

4. Jack LaLanne

5. Proctor Silex

6. Hurom

7. Samson

8. Green Star

9. Braun

10. Norwalk

Slow Cookers – New:

1. Instant Pot

2. All American

3. BLACK+DECKER

4. Tristar

5. Rival

6. Anova

7. Oster

8. Zojirushi

9. Crock-Pot

10. Tatung

Slow Cookers – Used:

1. Anova

2. Instant Pot

3. Zojirushi

4. All American

5. BLACK+DECKER

6. Mirro

7. Oster

8. West Bend

9. Presto

10. National

Water Filters – New:

1. Frigidaire

2. Whirlpool

3. LC

4. Kenmore

5. GE

6. PUR

7. Arrowpure

8. Samsung

9. Brita

10. Kinetico

Water Filters – Used:

1. Kangen

2. Berkey

3. ZeroWater

4. Brita

5. Pure

6. Waterwise

7. Kenmore

8. Amway

9. Aquasana

10. eSpring

Vacuum Flasks & Mugs – New:

1. Corkcicle

2. Yeti

3. ORCA

4. Rtic

5. Sowell

6. Contigo

7. Vera Bradley

8. Ozark Trail

9. BKR

10. Lilly Pulitzer

Vacuum Flasks & Mugs – Used:

1. Sowell

2. Takeya

3. Tervia

4. Stanley

5. Aladdin

6. Thermos

7. BKR

8. Yeti

9. Lifefactory

10. Pampered Chef

Hand Tool Sets - New:

1. Craftsman

2. Milwaukee

3. DEWALT

4. Kobalt

5. General Tools

6. IRWIN

7. Stanley

8. Allied

9. Crescent

10. PDR

Hand Tool Sets – Used:

1. Craftsman

2. Stanley

3. Armstrong

4. Paslode

5. Crescent

Drill Bits – New:

1. Craftsman

2. DEWALT

3. Klein Tools

4. Ryobi

5. Neiko

6. Milwaukee

7. Makita

8. Drill Master

9. Kreg

10. BLACK+DECKER

Socket Wrenches – New:

1. GearWrench

2. Craftsman

3. TEKTON

4. Flex

5. Stanley

6. Sunex

7. Snap-on

8. Neiko

9. Makita

10. STA-RITE

Socket Wrenches – Used:

1. Craftsman

2. Snap-on

3. Blue Point

4. SK

5. Huskey

6. Mac Tools

7. Cornwall

Impact Drivers - New:

1. Neiko

2. Milwaukee

3. Porter-Cable

4. DEWALT

5. Bosch

6. Bostitch

7. BLACK+DECKER

8. RIDGID

9. Drill Master

10. Craftsman

Impact Drivers – Used:

1. DEWALT

2. Milwaukee

3. Makita

4. PORTER-CABLE

5. Craftsman

6. Bostitch

7. Hilti

8. RIDGID

9. Hitachi

10. Ryobi'

Impact Wrenches – New:

1. Milwaukee

2. Craftsman

3. Ryobi

4. DEWALT

5. ACDelco

6. Kobalt

7. PORTER-CABLE

8. BALL

9. Trades Pro

10. RIGID

Impact Wrenches – Used:

1. Milwaukee

2. DEWALT

3. Ryobi

4. Snap-on

5. Makita

6. Craftsman

7. Bosch

8. Kobalt

9. Husky

10. SKIL

Power Tool Sets – New:

1. DEWALT

2. Craftsman

3. WORX

4. Milwaukee

5. Kobalt

6. Bostitch

7. Ryobi

8. RIDGID

9. SKIL

Power Tool Sets – Used:

1. WORX

2. Dewalt

3. Makita

4. Milwaukee

5. Ryobi

6. RIDGID

7. PORTER-CABLE

8. Craftsman

9. BLACK+DECKER

10. Shopsmith

Tool Bags, Belts & Pouches – New:

1. PORTER-CABLE

2. Milwaukee

3. DEWALT

4. VETO PRO PAC

5. Craftsman

6. Bosch

7. TOUGHBUILT

8. Husky

9. BLACK+DECKER

10. Makita

Tool Bags, Belts & Pouches – Used:

1. Klein Tools

2. Craftsman

3. AWP

4. Husky

5. VETO PRO PAC

6. McGuire-Nicholas

7. Milwaukee

8. CLC

9. Nicholas

10. BLACK+DECKER

Garden Flag Themes:

1. United States

2. Military

3. Seasonal

4. United Kingdom

5. Pirate

6. Thin Blue Line

7. Animals & Birds

8. States & Provinces

9. Advertising

BBQ Tools & Accessories – New:

1. Yoshi

2. Blackstone

3. Weber

4. Big Green Egg

5. Grillbot

6. Char-Broil

7. Snap-on

8. Brinkmann

9. Camp Chef

10. Hongso

BBQ Tools & Accessories – Used:

1. Pampered Chef

2. Brinkmann

3. Big Green Egg

4. Grillbot

5. Williams-Sonoma

6. Case

7. Weber

8. Mavericks

9. Coleman

Cat Flea & Tick Remedies:

1. Bayer

2. Seresto

3. Advantage

4. Vectra

5. Pet Armor

6. Nitenpyram

7. Sentry

8. CAPSTAR

9. Advocate

10. Hartz

Dog Flea & Tick Remedies:

1. Seresto

2. Nitenpyram

3. NexGard

4. CAPSTAR

5. Bayer

6. Advantix

7. Frontline

8. Bravecto

9. K9 Advantage

10. Maximum Defense

CHAPTER 11

JEWELRY

Jewelry is a hot seller on Ebay, both new and secondhand, especially vintage. Whether they are high-end items or unique handcrafted pieces, jewelry is a fun category to source for as you can find pieces at thrift stores (look for the jewelry jars at checkout if you like to dig for treasure), garage sales, and estate sales. Plus, jewelry is small, making it easy to photograph, list, store, and ship!

Fashion Bracelets – New:

1. Tory Burch

2. Kate Spade New York

3. Pura Vida

4. Lokai

5. Brighton

6. Kendra Scott

7. Hermosa

8. Handmade

9. Silpada

10. HERMES

Fashion Bracelets – Used

1. Brighton

2. ALEX AND ANI

3. Kate Spade New York

4. Silpada

5. Lagos

6. Stella & Dot

7. Coach

8. Louis Vuitton

9. HERMES

10. Michael Kors

Fashion Charms & Charm Bracelets – New:

1. Pandora

2. Origami Owl

3. Kate Spade

4. KEEP Collective

5. Brighton

6. Chanel

7. NOOSA

8. Juicy Couture

9. Waxing Poetic

10. Gingersnaps

Fashion Charms & Charm Bracelets – Used:

1. Pandora

2. Trollbeads

3. Brighton

4. Juicy Couture

5. James Avery

6. KEEP Collective

7. Gucci

8. Louis Vuitton

9. ALEX AND ANI

10. Charmed Memories

Fashion Earrings – New:

1. Tory Burch

2. Kate Spade New York

3. Kendra Scott

4. Chanel

5. Betsey Johnson

6. Brighton

7. J. CREW

8. Stella & Dot

9. Anthropolgie

10. BaubleBar

Fashion Earrings – Used:

1. Silpada

2. Kendra Scott

3. Brighton

4. Chanel

5. Pandora

6. Stella & Dot

7. Kate Spade New York

8. Tory Burch

9. Givenchy

10. Alexis Bittar

Fashion Necklaces & Pendants – New:

1. Kendra Scott

2. Prestige Cosmetics

3. Kate Spade New York

4. Tory Burch

5. Chanel

6. Sabika

7. Hermosa

8. Brighton

9. J. Jill

10. Stella & Dot

Fashion Necklaces & Pendants – Used:

1. Brighton

2. Kendra Scott

3. Stella & Dot

4. Silpada

5. J. Crew

6. Sabika

7. Kate Spade New York

8. Mine Finds by Jay King

9. Chico's

10. Judith Ripka

11. Alexis Bittar

Necklaces & Pendants – New:

1. Kendra Scott

2. Prestige Cosmetics

3. Kate Spade New York

4. Tory Burch

5. Chanel

6. Sabika

7. Hermosa

8. Brighton

9. J. Jill

10. Stella & Dot

Necklaces & Pendants – Used:

1. Brighton

2. Kendra Scott

3. Stella & Dot

4. Silpada

5. J. Crew

6. Sabika

7. Kate Spade New York

8. Mine Finds by Jay King

9. Chico's

10. Judith Ripka

Fashion Rings – New:

1. Kate Spade New York

2. Brighton

3. Handmade

4. Fragrant Jewels

5. Silpada

6. PANDORA

7. Michael Kors

8. Bella Luce

9. Coach

10. Betsey Johnson

Fashion Rings – Used:

1. Silpada

2. Pandora

3. Judith Ripka

4. Handmade

5. Diamonique

6. Michael Kors

7. Bella Luce

8. Brighton

9. Heidi Daus

10. Chanel

Fine Diamond Bracelets - New:

1. Cartier

2. David Yurman

3. Lagos

4. Van Cleef & Arpels

5. Diamondforgood

6. Affinity

7. IPPOLITA

Find Diamond Bracelets – Used:

1. David Yurman

2. Tiffany & Co.

3. Cartier

4. John Hardy

5. Charriol

6. Roberto Coin

7. Judith Ripka

8. Loui Vuitton

Fine Gemstone Bracelets – New:

1. David Yurman

2. Judith Ripka

3. Barbara Bixby

4. Lagos

5. John Hardy

6. Judith Jack

7. Mine Finds by Jay King

8. Van Cleef & Arpels

9. IPPOLITA

10. Tiffany & Co.

Fine Gemstone Bracelets – Used:

1. David Yurman

2. Judith Ripka

3. John Hardy

4. Carolyn Pollack

5. Silpada

6. Tiffany & Co.

7. IPPOLITA

8. Lagos

9. Jean Dousset

Fine Precious Metal Bracelets w/o Stones – New:

1. Cartier

2. David Yurman

3. Lagos

4. Tiffany & Co.

5. John Hardy

6. James Avery

7. Silpada

8. Pandora

9. Milor

10. Gucci

Fine Precious Metal Bracelets w/o Stones – Used:

1. David Yurman

2. Tiffany & Co.

3. James Avery

4. John Hardy

5. Silpada

6. Cartier

7. Lagos

8. Milor

9. Pandora

10. Lois Hill

Fine Charms & Charm Bracelets - New:

1. James Avery

2. OHM

3. Pandora

4. Trollbeads

5. Judith Ripka

6. Tiffany & Co.

7. Thomas Sabo

8. Adorable Charms

9. Barbara Bixby

10. Alex and Ani

Fine Charms & Charm Bracelets – Used:

1. James Avery

2. Kameleon

3. Pandora

4. Tiffany & Co.

5. Trollbeads

6. OHM

7. Disney

8. Lori Bonn Design

9. Kay Jewelers

10. Thomas Sabo

Fine Diamond Earrings – New:

1. Pompeii3

2. Kay Jewelers

3. Van Cleef & Arpels

4. Affinity

5. Diamondforgood

6. Roberto Coin

7. IPPOLITA

8. John Hardy

Fine Diamond Earrings – Used:

1. David Yurman

2. Tiffany & Co.

3. HERMES

4. Kay Jewelers

5. Zales

6. Roberto Coin

7. Chopard

8. John Hardy

9. Cartier

10. Judith Ripka

Fine Gemstone Earrings – New:

1. David Yurman

2. Judith Ripka

3. Judith Jack

4. Charles & Colvard

5. Pandora

6. IPPOLITA

7. Mine Finds by Jay King

8. Stephen Dweck

9. Maro Bicego

Fine Gemstone Earrings – Used:

1. David Yurman

2. Charles & Colvard

3. Judith Ripka

4. Silpada

5. Barbara Bixby

6. John Hardy

7. Lagos

8. Tiffany & Co.

9. IPPOLITA

Fine Earrings Precious Metal w/out Stones – New:

1. Tiffany & Co.

2. Pandora

3. Silpada

4. John Hardy

5. Lois Hill

6. Saudi Gold

7. Lagos

8. David Yurman

9. Gucci

Fine Earrings Precious Metals w/out Stones – Used:

1. James Avery

2. Tiffany & Co.

3. Silpada

4. David Yurman

5. John Hardy

6. Body Candy

7. Lagos

8. Milor

9. Lois Hill

10. Cartier

Fine Diamond Necklaces & Pendants – New:

1. Kay Jewelers

2. David Yurman

3. Van Cleef & Arpels

4. Roberto Coin

5. Jane Seymour

6. Effy

7. Pasquale Bruni

8. Meira T

9. Judith Ripka

Fine Diamond Necklaces & Pendants – Used:

1. David Yurman

2. Jane Seymour

3. Tiffany & Co.

4. Roberto Coin

5. Zales

6. Kay Jewelers

7. Cartier

8. John Hardy

9. Judith Ripka

10. Hearts on Fire

Fine Pearl Necklaces & Pendants – New:

1. Barbara Bixby

2. Honora

3. TASAKI

4. Mikimoto

5. Silpada

Fine Pearl Necklaces & Pendants – Used:

1. Mikimoto

2. Honora

3. David Yurman

4. Majorica

5. Silpada

6. Tiffany & Co.

7. James Avery

8. Lagos

9. Van Cleef & Arpels

10. Na Hoku

Fine Precious Metal Necklaces & Pendants w/out Stones – New:

1. Tiffany & Co.

2. David Yurman

3. James Avery

4. Pandora

5. John Hardy

6. Lagos

7. Silpada

8. Anna Beck

9. Helzberg

10. Bvlgari

Fine Precious Metal Necklaces & Pendants w/out Stones – Used:

1. James Avery

2. Tiffany & Co.

3. David Yurman

4. John Hardy

5. Silpada

6. Judith Ripka

7. Pandora

8. Barbara Bixby

9. Milor

10. Carolyn Pollack

Fine Diamond Rings – New:

1. Cartier

2. Kay Jewelers

3. David Yurman

4. Zales

5. LeVian

6. Tiffany & Co.

7. Helzberg

8. Afinity

9. Pompeii3

Fine Diamond Rings – Used:

1. David Yurman

2. Tiffany & Co.

3. Bvlgari

4. LeVian

5. Cartier

6. Kay Jewelers

7. Affinity

8. Hidalgo

9. Jane Seymour

Fine Gemstone Rings – New:

1. Pandora

2. David Yurman

3. Judith Ripka

4. Tiffany & Co.

5. Stephen Dweck

6. Lorenzo

7. John Hardy

8. Barbara Bixby

9. Or Paz

Fine Gemstone Rings – Used:

1. David Yurman

2. Cartier

3. Judith Ripka

4. Barbara Bixby

5. Carolyn Pollack

6. Epiphany

7. LeVian

8. James Avery

9. Ross Simons

10. Silpada

Fine Precious Metal Rings w/out Stones – New:

1. Tiffany & Co.

2. Bvlgari

3. Pandora

4. John Hardy

5. Brighton

6. Or Paz

7. Lagos

8. Silpada

9. Hidalgo

Fine Precious Metal Rings w/out Stones – Used:

1. James Avery

2. Tiffany & Co.

3. David Yurman

4. Pandora

5. Cartier

6. John Hardy

7. Silpada

8. Chrome Hearts

9. Kieselstein-Cord

Men's Bracelets:

1. Montblanc

2. Diesel

3. David Yurman

4. Black Jack

5. Miansai

6. John Hardy

7. Konstantino

8. Sabona

9. King Baby Studio

10. INOX

Men's Chains, Necklaces & Pendants:

1. Diesel

2. David Yurman

3. Harley-Davidson

4. Gucci

5. John Hardy

6. Chrome Hearts

7. King Baby Studio

Men's Cufflinks – New:

1. Bronkaid

2. Marvel

3. Gucci

4. Cartier

5. Montblanc

6. Montegrappa

7. Salvatore Ferragamo

8. Swank

9. Dior

10. David Yurman

Men's Cufflinks – Used:

1. Montblanc

2. Versace

3. Tiffany & Co.

4. Georg Jensen

5. Richard Krementz Gemstones

6. John Hardy

7. Salvatore Ferragamo

8. Dante

9. James Avery

10. Brooks Brothers

Men's Rings:

1. Harley-Davidson

2. John Hardy

3. David Yurman

4. Konstantino

5. Scott Kay

6. King Baby Studio

7. G&S

8. Tiffany & Co.

9. Triton

Watch Boxes, Cases & Winders – New:

1. Rolex

2. TAG Heuer

3. Invicta

4. Infantry

5. IWC

6. Breitling

7. Versa

8. Patek Philippe

9. Cartier

Watch Boxes, Cases & Winders – Used:

1. Rolex

2. Versa

3. Invicta

4. TUDOR

5. Breitling

6. Gucci

7. Cartier

8. Bulova

9. Citizen

10. Hamilton

Watch Wrist Bands – New:

1. Casio

2. Luminox

3. Nike

4. Michael Kors

5. Apple

6. G-SHOCK

7. Hublot

8. Seiko

9. OMEGA

10. Rolex

Watch Wrist Bands – Used:

1. Apple

2. OMEGA

3. Rolex

4. Panerai

5. Seiko

6. TAG Heuer

7. Nixon

8. Breitling

9. Nike

10. Casio

Wristwatches – New:

1. TechnoMarine

2. ESS

3. Michael Kors

4. Ruhla

5. G-SHOCK

6. Nixon

7. TW Steel

8. Invicta

9. Suunto

10. Luminox

Wristwatches – Used:

1. Caravelle New York

2. Swiss Army

3. Bulova

4. Seiko

5. Casio

6. Timex

7. Wittnauer

8. Frederique Constant

9. Invicta

10. G-SHOCK

CHAPTER 12

SPORTING GOODS

The Sporting Goods category on Ebay is huge and includes a lot of large items such as fitness machines and specialty parts. Thus, I've stuck to the things that you are most likely to find at garage sales and thrift stores that are also easy to ship.

Bicycle Lights & Reflectors:

1. LE

2. Schwinn

3. NiteRider

4. Garmin

5. Zefal

6. Cygolite

7. Fizik

8. CatEye

Fishfinders:

1. Humminbird

2. Klein Tools

3. Navionics

4. Lowrance

5. Garmin

6. Deeper

7. Lowrance

8. Eagle

Activity Trackers – New:

1. Fitbit

2. Moov

3. Under Armour

4. Misfit

5. Garmin

6. My Zone

7. Withings

8. Lumo

9. Spire

10. LEM

Activity Trackers – Used:

1. Fitbit

2. Samsung

3. Garmin

4. Microsoft

5. Basis

6. Lumo

7. Withings

8. My Zone

9. Jawbone

10. Under Armour

Men's Golf Shoes – New:

1. Oakley

2. Nike

3. FootJoy

4. Under Armour

5. ECCO

6. TRUE linkswear

7. Biion

8. G/FORE

9. New Balance

10. Sketchers

Men's Golf Shoes – Used:

1. Adidas

2. Nike

3. FootJoy

4. ECCO

5. PUMA

6. Callaway

7. Etonic

8. Oakley

9. Dexter

10. Under Armour

Golf Club Head Covers – New:

1. Bettinardi

2. Ping

3. Scotty Cameron

4. Odyssey

5. Callaway

6. Titleist

7. Nike

8. Cobra

9. TaylorMade

10. Disney

Golf Club Head Covers – Used:

1. Odyssey

2. Scotty Cameron

3. Ping

4. Mizuno

5. Bettinardi

6. YES

7. Callaway

8. SeeMore

9. TaylorMade

10. Rife

Golf Rangefinders & Scopes:

1. Bushnell

2. Garmin

3. Voice Caddie

4. Izzo Golf

5. Callaway

6. GolfBuddy

7. Nikon

8. SkyGolf

Golf Balls – New:

1. Titliest

2. Nike

3. Callaway

4. TaylorMade

5. Bandit

6. Precept

7. Dixon

8. Srixon

9. Bridgestone

Golf Balls – Used:

- Volvik
- Callaway
- Titleist
- Wilson Staff
- TaylorMade
- Bridgestone
- Nike
- Noodel

Baseball & Softball Gloves – New:

- Nike
- SSK
- Mizuno
- Easton
- Nokona

- Wilson

- Rawlings

- Miken

- Under Armour

- Worth

Baseball & Softball Gloves – Used:

- Rawlings

- Mizuno

- Wilson

- Nike

- Nokona

- Easton

- Louisville Slugger

- Worth

- SSK

- Spalding

Camping Ice Boxes & Coolers – New:

1. Rtic

2. Yeti

3. Arctic Zone

4. Ozark Trail

5. Blacks

6. Engel

7. ORCA

8. Igloo

9. Coleman

10. Pelican

Camping Ice Boxes & Coolers – Used:

1. Yeti

2. Coleman

3. Igloo

4. Thermos

5. Rubbermaid

6. Poloron

7. Outdoor Products

Camping Knives & Tools:

1. Leatherman

2. Supreme Performance

3. Gerber

4. Outdoor Products

5. Ganzo

6. Craftsman

7. Victorinox

8. Ozark Trail

9. Koch Tools

10. SOG

Camping Flashlights & Lanterns - New:

1. LumiTact

2. Bushnell

3. LE

4. Comunite

5. Shark

6. Atomic Beam

7. L&L

8. Hugsby

9. Foursevens

10. Stanley

Camping Flashlights & Lanterns – Used:

1. SureFire

2. Streamlight

3. Fenix

4. Mag-Lite

5. Brinkman

6. Nebo

7. Stanley

8. Coleman

9. NITECORE

10. Bushnell

Camping Headlamps:

1. Bushnell

2. L&L

3. UltraFire

4. Milwaukee

5. Black Diamon

6. HEAD

7. Energizer

8. Sky Wolf Eye

9. LE

10. Rayovan

Men's Football Cleats:

1. Under Armour

2. Nike

3. Joran

4. Adidas

5. New Balance

6. Reebok

Men's Soccer Clothing – New:

1. Umbro

2. Le coq sportif

3. Pirma

4. Nike

5. Adidas

6. Champion

7. Athletica

8. Under Armour

9. Lotto

10. Rhinox

Men's Soccer Clothing – Used:

1. Adidas

2. Nike

3. Official Sports

4. Umbro

5. Puma

6. Fila

7. Reebok

8. Atletica

9. Reusch

10. Kappa

Men's Soccer Shoes & Cleats – New:

1. Pirma

2. Nike

3. New Balance

4. Under Armour

5. Adidas

6. Lotto

7. Kelme

8. Diadora

9. Joma

10. Puma

Men's Soccer Shoes & Cleats – Used:

1. Nike

2. Adidas

3. Puma

4. Umbro

5. Under Armour

6. Lotto

7. Mizuno

CHAPTER 13

TOYS & HOBBIES

As I mentioned in the Introduction, this toy section was extremely hard to put together as the top selling toys change from month to month, and sometimes from week to week! As I'm writing this book, L.O.L. Surprise Dolls are one of the hottest Christmas toys; but there's no telling if they'll still be in by the time this book is printed. Therefore, I stuck to the more stable categories of comic book and television figures, which are actually purchased more for collecting than playing.

Vintage toys are a huge category and one that I sell a lot in; I will look up anything I find that was produced before the year 2000 to see how it is selling on Ebay. Licensed brands such as Disney, Marvel, Peanuts, and other cartoon character themes are always worth looking up. But, as with anything, condition is a huge factor in how much vintage toys will sell for.

Comic Book Heroes – New:

1. Spawn

2. Spiderman

3. Thanos

4. Marvel Legends

5. Marvel Universe

6. Fantastic Four

7. Lalaloopsy

8. X-Men

9. Justice League

10. Spider-Man

Comic Book Heroes – Used:

1. Marvel

2. Spiderman

3. Marvel Universe

4. Avengers

5. Thanos

6. Marvel Legends

7. Guardians of the Galaxy

8. X-Men

9. Lalaloopsy

10. Justice League

Designer & Urban Vinyl Figurines – New:

1. KAWS Companion

2. South Park

3. The Simpsons

4. Hello Kitty

5. Walking Dead

6. Futurama

7. Marvel Universe

8. Nightmare Before Christmas

9. Marvel

10. Bearbrick

Designer & Urban Vinyl Figurines – Used:

1. KAWS Companion

2. GI Joe

3. South Park

4. Street Fighter

5. The Simpsons

6. Futurama

7. Bearbrick

8. Dunny

9. Adventure Kartel

Military & Adventure Figures, Vehicles & Parts – New:

1. GI Joe

2. Big Jim

3. Elite Force

4. Star Wars

5. Ultimate Soldier

6. Superman

7. Action Man

8. Cobra Commander

9. Rambo

10. Halo

Military & Adventure Figures, Vehicles & Parts – Used:

1. GI Joe

2. Ultimate Soldier

3. Big Jim

4. Action Man

5. Johnny West

6. Brotherhood of Arms

7. Cobra Commander

8. Eagle Force

9. Military Muscle Men

10. Soldiers of the World

TV, Movie & Video Game Character Toys – New:

1. Jurassic World

2. Popeye

3. Guardians of the Galaxy

4. Jurassic Park

5. Marvel Universe

6. Fantastic Four

7. Animal Jam

8. Iron Man

9. Han Solo

10. Star Wars

TV, Movie & Video Game Character Toys – Used:

1. Jurassic Park

2. Star Wars

3. Halo

4. Masters of the Universe

5. Jurassic World

6. Iron Man

7. Power Rangers

8. Ewok

9. Thundercats

10. Princess Leia

Transformers & Robots – New:

1. Pokemon

2. Voltron

3. Transformers

4. Beast Wars

5. Robotech

6. Power Rangers

7. Gundam

8. Star Wars

9. Angry Birds

Transformers & Robots – Used:

1. Transformers

2. GI Joe

3. Voltron

4. Robotech

5. Macross

6. Star Wars

7. Power Rangers

8. Beast Wars

9. Gundam

LEGO Mini Figures – New:

1. Iron Man

2. Marvel

3. Lalaloopsy

4. The Incredible Hulk

5. Jurassic World

6. Avengers

7. Ant-Man

8. X-Men

9. Marvel Universe

10. The Incredibles

LEGO Mini Figures – Used:

1. Lalaloopsy

2. Iron Man

3. The Incredible Hulk

4. Star Wars

5. Ninjago

6. Teenage Mutant Ninja Turtles

7. Batman

8. Harry Potter

9. Spiderman

10. Ghostbusters

LEGO Complete Sets & Packs – New:

1. Boost

2. Jurassic World

3. Marvel Super Heroes

4. Factory

5. DC Comics Super Heroes

6. Dinosaurs

7. Star Wars

8. Mindstroms

9. Speed Champions

10. Ideas

LEGO Complete Sets & Packs – Used:

1. Cars

2. Star Wars

3. The Lord of the Rings

4. Ninjago

5. Bionicle

6. Pirates of the Caribbean

7. Disney Princess

8. SpongeBob SquarePants

9. Jurassic World

10. The Simpsons

Contemporary Diecast Aircraft Toys – New:

1. GeminiJets

2. Eagle

3. Forces of Valor

4. Hobby Master

5. RealToy

6. Atlas

7. Model Power

8. SkyMarks

9. Hogan

10. 21st Century Toys

Contemporary Diecast Aircraft Toys – Used:

1. GeminiJets

2. Franklin Mint

3. Hobby Master

4. 21st Century Toys

5. Armour

6. InFlight 200

7. Corgi

8. SkyMarks

9. Herpa

10. Dragon Wings

Contemporary Diecast Cars, Trucks & Vans – New:

1. Hot Wheels

2. Kyosho

3. Danbury Mint

4. Exoto

5. Hachette

6. Matchbox

7. Johnny Lightning

8. Ertl

9. Mattel

10. Die-Cast Promotions

Contemporary Diecast Cars, Trucks & Vans – Used:

1. Danbury Mint

2. Franklin Mint

3. New-Ray

4. Hot Wheels

5. Ertl

6. Greenlight

7. Johnny Lightning

8. Muscle Machines

9. Micro Machines

10. West Coast Precision

Vintage Diecast Cars, Trucks & Vans:

1. Smith Miller

2. Barclay

3. Exact Detail Replicas

4. Nylint

5. Tomy Pocket Cars

6. Hot Wheels

7. Tootsie Toy

8. Corgi Toys

9. Ertl

10. Politoys

Diecast NASCAR Cars by Driver – New:

1. Ryan Blaney

2. Chase Elliott

3. Martin Truex Jr.

4. Aric Almirola

5. Kyle Busch

6. Clint Bowyer

7. Brad Keselowski

8. Danica Patrick

9. Kevin Harvick

10. Courtney Force

Diecast NASCAR Cars by Driver – Used:

1. Kasey Kahne

2. Jimmie Johnson

3. Danica Patrick

4. Matt Kenseth

5. Dale Earnhardt

6. John Force

7. Dale Earnhardt Jr.

8. Kevin Harvick

9. Darrell Waltrip

10. Tony Stewart

Contemporary Board Games – New:

1. Jax

2. Game

3. Days of Wonder

4. Rich Dad

5. Hit

6. Cool Mini or Not

7. Mayfair Games

8. MMP

9. Nintendo

10. GMT

Contemporary Board Games – Used:

1. Rich Dad

2. Cool Mini or Not

3. Fantasy Fight Games

4. Milton Bradley

5. Avalon Hill

6. Hans im Gluck

7. Flying Frog Productions

8. GAME

9. Strat-O-Matic

10. Z-Man Games

Model Railroads & Trains HO Scale Freight Cars – New:

1. Red Caboose

2. Athearn

3. Branchline

4. Walthers

5. InterMountain

6. Roundhouse

7. Bowser

8. TYCO

9. IHC

10. Sunshine Models

Model Railroads & Trains HO Scale Freight Cars – Used:

1. Walthers

2. American Flyer

3. InterMountain

4. Atlas

5. Athearn

6. Accurail

7. Roundhouse

8. IHC

9. Rivarossi

10. Kadee

Model Railroads & Trains HO Scale Locomotives – New:

1. Athearn

2. Life-Like

3. Bowser

4. TYCO

5. KATO

6. Stewart

7. Walthers

8. Atlas

9. Bachmann

10. Lima

Model Railroads & Trains HO Scale Locomotives – Used:

1. Athearn

2. Atlas

3. Rivarossi

4. TYCO

5. Walthers

6. Bachmann

7. Mantua

8. Bowser

9. Life-Like

10. Lionel

Model Airplane Kits – New:

1. Monogram

2. 21st Century Toys

3. Revell

4. Wingnut Wings

5. F-Toys

6. Kitty Hawk

7. Testors

8. Tamiya

9. Ultimate Soldier

10. Sterling

Model Airplane Kits – Used:

1. Monogram

2. Revell

3. AMT

4. Accurate Miniatures

5. 21st Century Toys

6. Testors

7. MPC

8. Aurora

9. HobbyBoss

10. Special Hobby

Video Game Consoles – New:

1. Xbox One X $135

2. PlayStation 4 Pro $255

3. Nintendo Switch $51

4. Xbox One S $91

5. Nintendo Super NES Classic Mini $190

6. PlayStation TV $17

7. Nintendo NES Classic Edition $54

8. Gamecube $18

9. Xbox $35

10. Nintendo Classic Mini $62

Video Game Consoles – Used:

1. PlayStation 4 Slim $161

2. PlayStation 4 Pro $206

3. Xbox One X $123

4. Nintendo Switch $25

5. Game Boy Advance SP $44

6. PSP Go $83

BONUS

LIQUIDATION SOURCES

If you sell on Ebay, you already know that thrift stores and garage sales are where most resellers find the items they sell. Buying items secondhand for pennies on the dollar will always net you the greatest return on investment.

But what if you could have brand new inventory delivered right to your door? That's where liquidation comes in! Liquidation companies deal in a variety of merchandise, including:

1. Customer Returns

2. Shelf-Pulls

3. Overstocks

4. Surplus

5. Damaged Items

6. Store Clearance

Most liquidation companies sell items by the case, pallet or truckload; if you run your Ebay business out of your home, cases are the easiest to deal with as they ship in boxes. Pallets are delivered by a freight company and require a large space, such as a garage, to process. And I'm sure you can guess how much room a truckload takes up!

If you are looking into purchasing liquidation to resell on Ebay, it's important to research the companies to find out their policies and exactly what kinds of merchandise they sell. I personally only buy cases that are fully manifested (a print-out of each item including the brand, size and original MSRP) and that are in new condition. Note that "new" usually means that the original tags are still attached and that the item is unopened; these products may have been on the store shelves at one time and often come with clearance stickers on them, which you'll want to remove prior to listing.

You'll likely pay up a bit for liquidation items, but the cost makes up for not having to source the products yourself at numerous different locations. And if you purchase items that are new, you won't have to do any washing or repair. I wash all secondhand clothing before I list it on Ebay; but with liquidation, I just get straight to listing!

There are hundreds of liquidation companies out there; the following are the largest and best known. However, always do your own research before you order liquidation; just because a company is listed below doesn't mean it's a company that you will be happy with. My best advice is to start with a small case to test out a company so you can see if the items match their description, how the items are shipped, and what the customer service is like.

Note that you must register with each of these companies in order to see their prices and policies; some require that you provide a state sales tax permit in order to purchase from them. Creating accounts with these companies will get you on their mailing lists for new inventory alerts and special offers, too. Most offer a discount on your first order when you register an account with them.

B&G TRADING - https://bandgtrading.com/: B&G Trading specializes in overstock, shelf-pull and liquidation clothing from Macy's and Nordstrom's. They sell by both the case and the pallet.

BSTOCK.COM - https://bstock.com/: B-Stock connects you directly with liquidation sources at Amazon, Best Buy, Game Stop, GE, Lowe's, Macy's, Office Depot/Office Max, QVC, Walmart, Whirlpool, Sears, and JCPenney. Most of the sites they connect to are selling truckloads of merchandise via auction.

BULQ.COM - https://www.bulq.com/: Bulq.com sells liquidation from Target, Lowe's, and Bed Bath & Beyond; but the bulk of their items come from Target. They offer both cases and pallets with conditions of Brand New, Like New, Salvage, Scratch & Dent, and Uninspected Returns. Shipping on cases is $30; shipping on pallets is $200. They put up new lots every day, and they continuously mark them down until they sell. Bulq.com is a great source for cosmetics, toys, and consumer electronics.

CONTINENTAL WHOLESALE - https://continentalwholesale.com/: Located in Iowa, Continental Wholesale offers truck loads, half truck loads, and pallet lots of store liquidation from 16 different retailers.

DIRECT LIQUIDATION - https://www.directliquidation.com/: Direct Liquidation offers products from major retailers such as

Walmart, Target, Lowe's and Amazon in the form of auctions. They sell by the box, pallet and truckload.

EBAY - https://www.ebay.com/: You are selling on Ebay, but did you know you can source on Ebay, too? There are hundreds of liquidation lots for sale on Ebay at any given time. Just search "liquidation" or "reseller box" to see what is currently for sale.

ETSY - https://www.etsy.com/: If you are looking to buy vintage items or craft supplies in bulk to resell, try Etsy. There are sellers advertising "wholesale" and "reseller lots" of all sorts.

FOX LIQUIDATION - https://www.foxliquidation.com/: Fox Liquidation advertises wholesale clothing from brands such as Ralph Lauren, DKNY, Lacoste, Tommy Hilfiger, and more. They call their cases "small wholesale lots" and their pallets "wholesale lots". Their website also features a clearance section.

GOODWILL BLUEBOX - https://goodwillbluebox.com/: In 2019, Goodwill launched their "Bluebox" website, which sells lots of clothing that didn't sell in stores and was headed to one of their outlet locations. As of this writing, Goodwill Bluebox is very new and they sell out almost instantly whenever new stock launches. Hopefully they'll grow the program as it is an affordable way source potential Ebay inventory. It's worth it to sign up for their email list and to follow them on Instagram for inventory updates.

HONCHO WHOLESALE - https://honchowholesale.com/: Honcho Wholesale offers liquidation by the case and pallet. They mainly focus on clothing from Macy's, Nordstrom, and Nordstrom Rack. All of their lots are fully manifested so that you know exactly what you are buying.

LIQUIDATION.COM - https://www.liquidation.com/ : Liquidation.com offers a huge variety of goods to resell, including clothing, jewelry, electronics, computers, houseware, tools, and general merchandise. The twist is that the lots come from different sellers from across the country and are mostly available at auction. If you like hunting for deals, you'll love scrolling through Liquidation.com in search of lots to bid on.

LIQUIDATION GENERAL - https://www.liquidationgeneral.com/: Liquidation General specializes in high-end department store clothing. They also sell jewelry and specialty lots. Shipping on most of their lots appears to be free.

MERCHANDIZE LIQUIDATORS - https://www.merchandizeliquidators.com/: Merchandize Liquidators specializes in truckloads and pallets of cosmetics, clothing, housewares, and more. You can visit their headquarters in Miami Gardens, Florida, or buy from them online.

MIDTENN WHOLESALE - https://midtennwholesale.com/: Run by former Ebay sellers, MidTenn Wholesale sells a variety of merchandise from various sources in conditions ranging from brand new to salvage. Their lots are at a fixed price and range from cases to truckloads.

POSHMARK – https://poshmark.com/: Poshmark is an app (it's also accessible via computer) where people can buy and sell clothing. There is a whole community of Poshmark resellers; and some of them also offer wholesale/liquidation lots for sale. Try typing "liquidation", "wholesale", or "reseller lot" into the search bar to see what is available. Since Poshmark offers flat $6.95 Priority Mail shipping on packages weighing five pounds or less, expect to only find smaller lots for sale. But, again, it's an affordable way to test liquidation or buying in bulk.

QUICKLOTZ.COM - https://www.quicklotz.com/: Quicklotz offers cases, pallets and truckloads at set prices that ship from three warehouses across the United States. They also sell Mystery Cases that ship for free within the Continental United States.

SOURCE LIQUIDATION - https://liquidation.source.com/: Source Liquidation is a liquidation marketplace that connects businesses with excess merchandise to resellers. All listings are auctions.

THREDUP – http://www.thredup.com/r/1W7XCF: While not a traditional liquidation company, ThredUp, which is on online consignment store, sells "Rescue" boxes. These mystery box lots contain items that weren't accepted for consignment or items that were listed but didn't sell. They offer clothing, handbags, shoes, and jewelry. You can also buy from them in bulk; email them at buybulk@thredup.com for more information.

VIATRADING - https://www.viatrading.com/: With lots starting at only $100, ViaTrading is a great option for testing out liquidation. They sell everything from brand new cosmetics to salvage appliances. If you are in the Los Angeles, California, area, you can even visit their warehouse and purchase pallets in person. They also have weekly on-site auctions.

WHOLESALE NINJAS - https://wholesaleninjas.com/: Wholesale Ninjas sells liquidation by the case, pallet and truckload. They mainly sell cosmetics, toys, and clothing from Target and CVS. With box lots starting at around $100, Wholesale Ninjas offers an affordable way to test liquidation.

CONCLUSION

I hope that after reading this book you are excited to go sourcing for Ebay! Just researching this book opened my eyes up to so many opportunities that I've been passing by. From clothing brands that I once turned my nose up at to consumer electronics I thought I wasn't knowledgeable enough to resell, I'm now going into thrift stores and estate sales excited for all of the new brands I've learned about.

Again, as I've said several times throughout this book, always do your own research before buying items to sell. There are literally hundreds of different categories on Ebay. While this book covered the most popular, there are always more subcategories being added and new brands, styles, and genres to learn about. With Ebay, as with all retail, what is hot today may be a big NOT tomorrow.

Whether you sell in one category or in multiple, I sincerely hope this book gave you some new ideas of items to sell on Ebay!

ABOUT THE AUTHOR

Ann Eckhart is a writer, blogger, YouTube creator, social media influencer, and Ebay seller based in Iowa. She has written numerous books about selling on Ebay, saving money, and making money online. Check out her Amazon Author Page at https://amzn.to/2B99zFL for all of her titles.

You can keep up with everything Ann does on her blog at www.AnnEckhart.com. You can also connect with her on the following social media networks:

FACEBOOK: https://www.facebook.com/anneckhart/

TWITTER: https://twitter.com/ann_eckhart

INSTAGRAM: https://www.instagram.com/ann_eckhart/

YOUTUBE CHANNEL: https://www.youtube.com/c/AnnEckhart

If you enjoyed this book, please be sure to leave it a 5-star review on Amazon: https://amzn.to/2B99zFL